SHINE THROUGH THE DARKNESS

Reignite Christ's Light in your Life

Gavin Van Moer

I would like to thank my beautiful wife Kimberly for all of her love and support. None of this is possible without her.
Love you, sweetheart,

This little light of mine
I'm going to let it shine
Let it shine, all the time, let it shine

Harry Dixon Loes

*All Bible quotes in this book are from the NRSV Catholic Edition

Contents

Introduction 4
    My faith Journey 6
    Are you Catholic? 11
Know God 15
    Where do we find God? 19
    Choosing God 23
    First Step 25
    5 Minutes 29
    Reading the Bible 34
    Personal Relationship with God 39
    Advent and Christmas 43
    Lent 53
    Does God Know You? 61
Love God 66
    How to Pray 73
    Forgiveness 82
    Forms of Prayer 90
    Heaven on Earth 98
    Suffering and Doubt 103
Serve God 111
    Fear 113
    The Rich Man and Lazarus 121
    Sharing the Faith 125
    As I Have Done For You 133
    SHINE! 136
Epilogue 144

Introduction

When I was a senior in High School, I faced the reality of death for the first time when my grandfather passed away. It was the first time I had ever lost anyone close to me. I loved my grandfather and the emotions of losing him were hard to handle. You start to realize you won't see his truck driving around the section on a late fall evening, or see him show up in his best suit to Sunday Mass. You start to realize what you might have taken for granted when you lose someone for the first time.

My relationship with my grandfather was better than I could have asked for. Growing up, we only lived a mile from the family farm where my grandparents lived, and during the summer I would bike down there every morning. We would go out in the field to pick rocks and help Grandma in the garden. Then after lunch, he would start yelling at Grandma for cheating in card games. He would drive me to baseball practice, and out to lunch at the local Dairy Queen. My grandfather was a man of few words, but you never questioned his love and support for you.

By the time I had graduated from college and had moved away from home, I began working on my first book *"1910, Building a Legacy"*. This book focuses on my paternal family history, and a large portion focuses on my grandfather's time in the Army. When my Grandfather was in the Army, he wrote back home to his father, and luckily all those letters were saved. I started going through each letter individually and transcribing them onto a Word document to preserve his writings.

With each letter, I was fascinated to read about my grandfather's experiences. To hear about the people in his barracks, the maneuvers they would execute, and of course, the sights he saw while in Europe. As I kept reading each letter, I started to get a new understanding of my grandfather, and it dawned on me that he was the same age writing those letters as I was reading them. The more I learned about his work ethic and no-quit attitude, I started to realize that if we grew up at the same time, we probably would have been best friends. This is the same man that I spent hours cruising along the countryside, in that quiet truck, thinking how different we were, only to find out that I just never really got to know who he was.

How often do we tend to just spend time with the people we love, or the people closest to us, but don't truly build that relationship with each other? How often do we put our lives on cruise control and spend each day going through the motions to get through another week? I started to realize that if we can so easily walk through life without genuinely knowing the people around us, who else do we neglect?

Now the grand question is this: How is our relationship with God? Do we make an effort to get to know who God is, or do we take his love for granted? I'm sure a lot of us think of God as the old guy in the sky who we know loves us but is quiet and sometimes hard to talk to.

In this book, my goal is to present the three easy steps that every Catholic and Christian should do to continue building their relationship with God. Whether you are a practicing Catholic, someone who has lost your faith in the church, or even someone who has never had a relationship with God, this book is for all of us.

We are all sinners looking for happiness in life, but are we willing to make that effort daily, or when it is all said and done, will we look back on our lives and think "I never knew who God was"?

My Faith Journey

I was born and raised in Tracy, MN into a wonderful Catholic family. My parents, grandparents, great-grandparents, and so on, all shared the same faith. It was truly a blessing and without a doubt built me into the man I am today. Growing up in a small town, surrounded by family, showed me how I wanted to raise future generations. I also was blessed with the opportunity to attend Catholic grade school and it formed a strong community around me. It developed a love for my faith and created friendships that are still just as strong today. This community taught me how to become a practicing Catholic and how to grow in my faith.

I attended Mass twice a week throughout grade school and with my family. When I got to High School, I went to Wednesday night faith formation. I received all of my sacraments of Baptism, Reconciliation, Eucharist, and Confirmation by the time I graduated high school. I was lucky enough to get confirmed as a junior which meant no more faith formation on Wednesdays during my senior year. With Wednesday nights open, it would have been easy to just use the free night to relax at home and watch TV, but I knew I was called to do more with my faith. I had just received the beautiful sacrament of Confirmation and I wanted to share my passion for my faith. I still had the desire to participate in the St. Mary's faith formation, but now as a teacher. That year, I taught our second-grade class and of course, that meant walking these kids through their first Reconciliation and first communion. It was incredible to be able to watch these young kids take such an important step in their faith and to see their excitement about receiving the sacraments.

After high school, I went to South Dakota State University where I studied Education with a specialization in History. Now, this isn't the moment where I lose my faith, get lost in alcohol, and make a miraculous re-conversion back into my faith, but yet it was almost something much worse on a spiritual level. I attended Mass on Sunday and considered that good enough. The day-to-day practices of my faith began to wither.

One aspect of my faith that remained steady was my strong desire to defend my faith and would listen to apologetics on certain topics. While my daily prayer and devotion to my faith got weaker, the college experience did strengthen the defense of my faith. It shouldn't come as a surprise to anyone, but part of the college experience is the large mixing pot of different beliefs, theories, and ideologies. This can cause some unique dialogue when differing opinions meet in a classroom discussion. I can genuinely say that my freshman year was the first time I ever had to defend my beliefs. Obviously, not all of my friends were Catholic in high school but we were all Christians and didn't worry about what each other did on Sundays because it didn't affect us. That all changes when some strangers start yelling at you in a philosophy class when you say that human euthanasia is wrong.

These objections to my beliefs caused me to have a rush of motivation in diving into apologetics, and then as the passion dwindled, I would get back to the minimum requirement of my spiritual practices. I was just going through the motions to keep up with the image of who I wanted people to think I was. I had gone my whole life with a structured faith around me that I trained myself how to be a Catholic instead of living as one.

We all need to get to that moment in our lives where we realize that the relationship with God can get fairly one-sided. I will use this comparison a lot but if I just went through the motions in my marriage and didn't put any effort into learning about my wife or communicating with her, our marriage would crumble and we would just become roommates that tolerate each other. We must understand that Christianity is not mechanical but a relationship with God. We build our relationship with God the same way we build our human relationships through understanding, communication, and selflessness. So once again, I ask, how is your relationship with God today, and where do you want it to be?

I am a sinner, and certainly not a philosopher. There are so many podcasts and brilliant authors that do this for a living. 2,000 years of saints and scholars, I'm sure everything has already been said before, hasn't it? So why am I writing this book? To keep it simple because of my wife. Like I said I grew up Catholic and knew all the right answers to anyone's questions, but it was because of my wife who was raised as a protestant, that I finally spiritually woke up.

It is safe to say that our relationship grew quickly. From the time we went on our first date, to when I proposed it wasn't even 5 months. During that span, our conversations developed into a serious dialogue about our past, our goals for the future, and of course, our faith.

Like most conversations between Catholics and Protestants, we had a lot in common, and for anything that we differed on, we discussed what the two sides believed in. As we dated I continued to take her to Mass and I could see her curiosity begin to grow in the faith. As our relationship got more serious, the talk of marriage started to make its way into the conversation which led to the big question "Where are we going to get married?" It was then, that we decided that our future was in the Catholic church and that we should get married in the Catholic church.

As we started to begin preparations for the big day, we still had to go through the pre-marriage classes for the church. Although she wouldn't be confirmed into the faith before our wedding, the lessons learned during these classes helped us form our faith as a couple instead of as individuals.

Then after our marriage, she started the RCIA program (Rite of Christian Initiation of Adults), and would be confirmed the following Spring. It was at the RCIA program that I received my wake-up call.

I started to realize that I was weak when it came to my knowledge of scripture, my prayer life was non-existent, and although I volunteered with teaching, all of my time was focused on my career and not my community. I realized that at 25 years old, I was just walking through the motions of my faith and didn't have a direction for where it was going.

Becoming a husband and a father made me realize that I needed to be an example for my domestic church. If I want my family to have a personal relationship with God every day, our faith formation must start at home. We are introduced to and inspired to live out our faith by the example our parents and grandparents show us. I am the first to say, I was spoiled to grow up where each Sunday, I would go to church and my family would fill out a whole pew from Grandpa down to me. I sympathize with those that didn't have a domestic church to grow up in and discovered the faith as they grew up.

We all have challenges in our lives and our faith journeys. Some of us have lost our faith, and others maybe have never been introduced to God, to begin with. The beauty of God's love for us is that no matter how far off the path we get he is always waiting for us to come home, and will graciously receive us with loving arms. So as you begin this journey to building your relationship with God, I want you to start by forgiving yourself and letting down your burdens. Allow yourself to be loved and from this day forward, focus on your future with God and keep an eye on your Heavenly destination.

Are you Catholic?

Now, this isn't the point of the book where I point out that if you're not Catholic then you're in the wrong place. It's the exact opposite, and I hope that my efforts in the book reach out to more than just Catholics but to all Christians. Even though I will talk a lot about my Catholic faith, what is expected of us as Catholics, and what is God's plan for us. The goal of this book is simply to show a 3 step plan on how we can all develop our relationship with God. Now, I will give specific examples that are solely Catholic, and hopefully, people that read this, are encouraged at least to dive into the Catholic faith and what she offers.

Now to the Catholic readers, I am specifically asking you to do some self-evaluation as you begin reading. I want you to look at your current relationship with God and ask yourself, do you see yourself as a practicing Catholic or do you just go through the motions? Do you make an effort to go to church every Sunday, regardless of where you are or do you find the smallest excuse to skip Mass? This isn't me trying to get you to feel guilty about how you live your spiritual life but if you genuinely want to grow in your faith, you need to have a healthy starting point. Just like if I was trying to lose weight, I need to self-evaluate my bad habits first if I want to have any chance of obtaining my goal.

A lot of the time, we hear the term 'cradle Catholic' thrown around, this is a term designated to identify someone who was born, baptized, and raised in the Catholic faith. Depending on how you use it, this can be both positive and negative. I am what you would consider a 'cradle Catholic' and there have been different times in my life when I have been on both sides of the term.

Being born in the faith is an incredible blessing and lays a foundation for you. You are born into a community full of love and devotion to Christ, the saints, and the community. Where it turns negative is when we become complacent and lazy with our beliefs. We become Catholic only by name and not by action. This is when we find ourselves just going through the motions in life, at Mass, and never really asking ourselves the "why" of what we are doing.

I will be the first to confess that I am a sinner and continually fall back into the same sins. Just because I am writing this book, doesn't mean I am this holy man without flaws. The church isn't built up of perfect saints, but the pews are filled with sinners striving to be saints. Pope Francis said *"The church is not a museum of saints, but a hospital for sinners."*[1]

---

[1] Justin McLellan, Catholic News Service, Catholic News Service Cindy Wooden, Nicole Winfield, and Pat Marrin. "The Church Should Be a Hospital for Sinners." National Catholic Reporter.

When I was a kid I had a habit of sleepwalking occasionally. I was never aware of it, but I would wander around the house, and usually just be creepy or weird. I would always wake up where I fell asleep and have no recollection of the events that took place. Now I wouldn't trash the house like you see in the movie *Step Brothers*, but I had no control over my actions.

When I was maybe around 10 years old I was sleepwalking through the house, and my older siblings decided they would have some fun with it. They would talk to me, and start giving me instructions to do. I was like a robot and would do everything they commanded. Probably the funniest occasion was when they got me to put my shoes on, grab my backpack, and told me to go wait for the school bus because I was going to be late for school. Well, it was the middle of the night, it was the weekend, 0 and it was the middle of the summer but there was no rationality going on in my head. My mother wasn't too impressed and they helped get me back to bed.

It's crazy to think of how easy it is for someone to control you when you are sleepwalking. Now think of areas in our lives where we are sleepwalking, or going through the motions like our faith. When we aren't in control of our faith, and the direction of our life, then who is? How easy is it for the devil and all his temptations to lure you to a dangerous place, and lead you to make a decision that could destroy your life or the relationships in it? Even worse we could sleepwalk through our whole lives blocking out God and find ourselves lost when we finally wake up. It is time to take control of your life. It is time to wake up and take action.

So ask yourself, where are you on your faith journey today? Are you a part of the over 70% of Catholics, that are Catholic by name only and don't hold the core teachings of the faith? Are you a practicing Catholic who wants to continue growing in your faith, or are you from outside of the faith just trying to figure us crazy Catholics out? Are you someone who is seeking a stronger relationship with God and don't know where to begin? If so, let me show you the simple 3 step plan that helped me build my relationship with God through my family, and why I love being Catholic.

Know God

Who is God anyway, and what does a relationship with Him even look like? For many, when we ask who God is, the first thing that comes to mind is an old bearded guy, sitting up in the clouds watching over us. Although this makes it easier to try and picture God, it is far from the truth. For starters, although God is referred to as our Father, the reality is that God is neither man nor woman. God is an eternal spirit who exists outside of time itself. No beginning and no end. God is an eternal source of life, and as we will continuously talk about in this book, love.

So if God is this great and powerful spirit then how can we have a connection with God? Well, let us go to the beginning, of course. What separates humans from other animals on Earth? We are made in the image and likeness of God (Gen 1:26). No other creature on Earth is given this honor. From our beginning, God has always had a special connection with His people. When God created us, He always intended for us to live side by side with Him in paradise. This did not last due to the fall.

When Adam and Eve first sinned, it created a divide between God and His people. Our first parents showed a lack of trust in God and disobeyed him; a mistake that is made throughout all of human history and is still made today. Now the intercession of sin drove humans away from God more than simply, God abandoning His people. We see evidence of that throughout the Old Testament. The chosen people of God continuously live lives of sin where they are filled with murder, war, greed, and idolizing false gods. If God truly wanted to abandon us, He never would have formed a covenant with the Israelites. The entirety of the Old Testament is a rollercoaster of the chosen people falling in and out of faith in God.

The prime example of this is the Exodus. After God frees the chosen people from 400 years of slavery under the Egyptians, they rejoice, but once they begin wandering, they start to lose their faith. In the book of Exodus, we hear the Israelites begin to complain.

> *The whole congregation of the Israelites complained against Moses and Aaron in the wilderness. The Israelites said to them, 'If only we had died by the hand of the Lord in the land of Egypt, when we sat by the fleshpots and ate our fill of bread; for you have brought us out into this wilderness to kill this whole assembly with hunger.'*
>
> *Exodus 16:2-3*

Even though they had been freed from slavery after 400 years, they grew frustrated after nearly two months of freedom. We still haven't stopped complaining today.

How often do we take things for granted? When we are kids, how often would we give anything for our parents to get us something small like a candy bar, or a baseball card?

Nothing else in the world would make you happier. Then once you get it, the excitement wears off. "Oh, but when I get older and I get a car, then my life will be complete." "When I get the promotion, I won't have to ask for anything." It's human nature to seek satisfaction. In some ways, it can be positive, where we push ourselves harder to obtain the goals in our lives, but the majority of the time, this trait leads us to live lives of jealousy, greed, and judgment. We begin focusing on what we don't have instead of being gracious with what we do have. Our world has become so materialistic that we only focus on how much stuff we can accumulate to make us happy. How often do we take the simpler path and understand we don't need much in life to make us happy?

When I graduated from college, I didn't use my degree but instead followed in my father's footsteps in the sow management industry running a gestation/ farrowing barn. I chose this path because I could see a life of growth, promotions, and success. For the first few years, I got all of that. In under 2 years, I went from power washing pig pens to managing a 3,000-head sow farm where we would produce over 90,000 wean pigs in a year. I became the youngest manager in this company's history and the success made me "happy".

At the time I wasn't in any relationships, I lived in a cheap basement apartment that smelled like sewage because the pipes would back up. I continually reminded myself that I was "happy" because I was getting all the promotions I wanted and someday down the road, I will have all the "stuff" I need to make up for this time in a dinky apartment.

My whole world changed one weekend when I saw a beautiful girl dancing to a 'Meatloaf' song (I know it's truly romantic). When I met my wife, no longer was my work the number one priority in my life. For the first time in my life, I had someone else to think about, and new goals to prioritize. It was no longer what makes me happy but what makes US happy. It showed me that I didn't need the promotions, but all I needed was this woman to make me truly happy. This woman that God has blessed me with is all that I will ever need.

The one thing that every human on Earth has in common, regardless of age, race, gender, income bracket, or where they live is we are all looking for happiness. Chris Stefanick's program *'The Search'* series, does a phenomenal job at honing in on this idea.[2] If you watch TV, the advertisements will tell you what you NEED to make you happy. New vehicles, fancy vacations, the newest iPhone, ect. When we live our lives trying to fill that void of happiness in ourselves with material goods, we are just like the Israelites and never satisfied.

How often on day 5 of a vacation has the fun worn off and you just want to be home? Or after driving a new vehicle for a few weeks, the shine has worn off and you are still left making the payments for 4-5 years. Just like when we overindulge in our family's Thanksgiving meal it doesn't matter how miserable we make ourselves feel by cramming as much food in our bellies, you will still be hungry

---

[2] *The Search*. Augustine Institute, 2022. https://www.thesearch begins.org/.

tomorrow. The material goods of this Earth can never eternally satisfy our hunger for happiness.

We all have a God-sized hole inside us, and we keep trying to fill it with something else. So when we ask the question, "Who is God?", the answer is simple. God is Love, God is Happiness, and God is Everlasting. God is our creator and He wants to build a relationship with YOU.

Where do we find God?

My wife and I teach high school religious education on Wednesday nights for our local parish. At the beginning of every year, we always begin with the same question, "Why are you Catholic?" A similar start to how we began this book. The reason I like to start with this is because I can assume for most young teenagers, this is a question that they have never been asked. They have never had to defend their faith, or even question what or why they believe in Catholic teachings. I emphasize this because especially for small-town kids when they move off to a bigger city or college, this will be the biggest test of their faith they may ever face, and I fear they aren't prepared.

The responses are what you might think. "My family is Catholic" … "I was Baptized Catholic" … "I don't know why", are all common answers that we will receive, and trust me, none of them are wrong. Ask yourself the same question and what would your response be? When I was in high school I would have said, "Because I always have been." Our faith has to be more than just a passed-down tradition but true ownership and love for the faith. Everything about who we are spiritually is about God.

Now the challenge for a teenager is they may not have had that big experience with God yet, or maybe no one has shown them truly who He is. As mentioned before, we all run the risk of sleepwalking through our faith.

The discussion always gets interesting when we ask the follow-up question, "Where is God?" The first answer is always, "In church … In the Eucharist … In all of us." Absolutely correct, but let's look closer at his presence. How do we learn about God? "The Bible … Catholic authors … Educational videos." Alright, how about entertainment? "Well Christian music … Christian movies … Catholic speakers or podcasts." Now we're talking, but what about people? "Priests and nuns … parents and grandparents … teachers and neighbors." How about when we are on our phones? "We have catholic apps … Youtube videos … daily bible quotes."

So when we dive deeper, we can start to see that God is all around us, but that's nothing overly groundbreaking. Then let's ask the question, "Where isn't He allowed?" "Lots of movies … popular music … Tik Tok … School … Celebrities … Internet … Friends." It's always fascinating how much easier it is for the kids to identify where God is absent. This shouldn't be a surprise because pop culture and mainstream media don't want God in their content and everyone knows teenagers love what's popular.

So now that we have looked at where God is and where He isn't, let's compare our lists;

God is here	**No God here**
Christian Music	Popular Music
Christian Movies	Hollywood Movies
Priests and nuns	Celebrities and Influencers
Podcast	Podcast
Books	Books
Catholic Apps	Tik Tok
Social Media	Social Media
Friends	Friends

    Now let's analyze the data. Very fascinating because it appears our list is identical. Now certainly that could just be a mistake and we aren't thinking hard enough about the question, or the real answer is simpler than we would like to accept.

    God is everywhere, but do we make the effort to invite Him into our lives? To keep it simple, we all have to CHOOSE to see God. When we are looking for entertainment, do we look at the top 50 rap songs about getting drunk and going to the club, to sleep around? Or do we find an uplifting song, or listen to a hymn? Do we listen to Catholic apologetics and speakers to learn about our faith or allow atheists to form doubt in our minds about how irrational it is to believe in a God when science is all you need? Do we follow the examples of faith leaders like priests and sisters, or are we easily influenced by what crazy ½ naked celebrities or influencers on Instagram are doing? Do we use apps to fill us with knowledge about God's teaching and assist us in our prayer lives, or watch girls dancing in revealing clothes on Tik Tok? Do we surround ourselves with supportive friends who support our faith, or friends who don't want to waste their time with all this God stuff?

Life is all about choices. Harvard, Social Psychologist, Dr. David McClelland was known for his theory that, "the people you habitually associate with determine as much as 95 percent of your success or failure in life".[3] The people and the environment we surround ourselves with are all choices that we make on a day-to-day basis and will impact our life going forward. Motivational speaker, Jim Rohn was quoted saying, "You are the average of the five people you spend the most time with."[4] Now I think it is safe to say where society is at now, our phones would take up a few of those slots.

So what are your goals in life? Who do you want to be, and who do you want to become? Do you strive to be a better person who is charitable, reliable, and faith-centered? Do you want to build a foundational relationship with God? Then it is time to make the choice. Is God going to be in your top 5?

---

[3] Van Doorn, Maarten. "The Height of Your Potential Is Predicted by the People Who Surround You." Medium, October 16, 2019.

[4] Ibid

Choosing God

When I was in high school, my parents took me up to the boundary waters in northern Minnesota. To explain the boundary waters is as simple as saying, "Hop in your time machine and go back a few hundred years". Gorgeous natural habitats, and untouched wilderness. Endless forests filled with wildlife, and crystal clear lakes filled with life. The sights and the sounds are by far the most beautiful in our state. The most beautiful part is how simple life is up there. No internet, no cell phones, and nowhere to be. You get to step into a world where time isn't a factor and truly find peace.

The challenging part is always getting there. For us, living in southwest Minnesota, it is an 8-hour drive just to get up to the northern part of the state. After a night of rest, you rise early to get out on the water as soon as you can. When my parents brought me, our destination was usually around 6 miles into the boundary waters. 6 miles of paddling through lakes, creeks, and portaging through the forest to reach your camp. Sometimes it would take numerous trips to move all the food, canoes, and backpacks through the trails. Hours of physical work to reach a simple campsite on the shore of a lake, but yet you never seemed to complain. The beauty around you, and the promise of the perfect campsite on the lake kept you going. It was always so rewarding to spend that first night gathered around a campfire, watching the setting sun reflect across the water.

Our spiritual lives can be just as beautiful. We never really think of our lives as much of a journey but more of a challenge that we have to endure. Maybe we even look at it as a competition when we start comparing ourselves to others. How often do we go through our lives feeling lost and defeated? Do we ever lose sight of where we are heading in life, or do we get sucked into all the day-to-day distractions?

When we are young, we all dream about going to Heaven, but as we get older, we let life get in the way. We start to take new priorities and lose focus on what is truly important. When life becomes challenging we tend to make excuses, complain, and feel sorry for ourselves. We all are dealt our challenges and trials in this life and that's what makes the journey ours. It is up to us to decide how we respond to adversity. When we look at the lives of the saints, I can't find a single one who had an easy life, or who coasted their way into sainthood. They all lived challenging lives where they were persecuted, mocked, and even killed.

Paramahansa Yogananda, a Hindu monk, was quoted saying, "A saint is a sinner who never gave up."[5] Is it as clear as mud yet?

It would be wonderful if we could all just hop on an interstate with a straight shot to Heaven. No obstacles, difficulties, or breaks but that's not reality. Just like venturing through the boundary waters, we are going to venture through deep forests, narrow creeks, and rough waters as we follow the path to get to our final destination.

Just like in life, there is a path laid before us to follow, but it is up to us to stay true to the path that God has provided. It is easy for us to venture off and get lost, but we

---

[5] Yogananda, Paramahansa. "Paramahansa Yogananda Quote: 'A Saint Is a Sinner Who Never Gave Up.'" Quotefancy.

must remember that we are never alone. It would be irresponsible of me to venture through dangerous terrain by myself, and God understands it's too dangerous to venture through life alone. When we journey with God and get ourselves lost, He will patiently wait for us to return. When we are lost, we can hear Him calling us out by name searching for us until we safely return to the path to righteousness.

We are all on this journey together and never alone. Take a quick moment to pause and listen. Is God calling your name? Are we lost on our way to salvation? Will we continue deeper into the woods where we can no longer hear God's voice, or continue to fight our way back towards him? We all must make that choice. Increase your exposure to God and you will begin to hear His voice. As we begin this faith journey, you will soon be walking side by side with God, and someday you will sit with Him in paradise watching the sunset on your journey.

First Step

Taking that first step is probably the hardest because we are admitting to ourselves that we need to make a change. The entire Catholic faith is focused on making personal changes. We will use the term repent a lot. Most Catholics think that repenting is just a formal word for "I'm sorry God", but that's not it at all. We get the word repent from the Greek word metanoia, which means to change one's mind or thinking.[6] We are all going to be starting this change at different stages in our lives. Some of us may just be entering college, and are constantly falling in and out of our faith, some might have always been faithful but have just lost sight of what a daily commitment to God looks like.

Now when we talk about building a relationship with God our end goal isn't that we all become priests and nuns, but that we all have that personal relationship with God that leads us all to our vocation. The challenge is always how unique our own lives are. It would be easy to copy and paste a 3-step plan into your own life and then BAM you are saved. We know that's not true because we are all different whether it's male, female, old, young, single, married, widowed, blue collar, high rollers, or whatever makes us unique in our own way.

Regardless of who we are and where we are beginning this journey, we all need to make the same first step. Invite God into your life. I'm not asking you to sign your name on the dotted line, and if you break the agreement, you are now banned from the church. Simply, if we have turned away from God, the first step is to turn toward him and invite him into our life.

I guarantee when we were all young, we all had a similar situation where we broke a dish, or a rule and somehow knew we were going to be in trouble. What was our response as children? Well if I cover it up, maybe my parents

---

[6] "Metanoia Definition & Meaning." Merriam-Webster.

won't notice, or if I hide in my room while they are mad, by the time they get to me, maybe they will have already moved on from it. How childish are we in our spiritual lives to think that God is a mean parent ready to scold us because we have failed? We are all shameful of our sinful lives, but instead of turning towards God and asking, "Help me", we hide and say "How could He ever love me?"

When we sin we immediately try to cover it up and pretend like nothing is happening. The last thing we want is for people to know that we are imperfect. We then hide from God because we anticipate that He will be angry with us. It would just be best for us to disappear. To hide away deeper into the darkness.

God isn't like that though. God, isn't this mean parent standing on top of the staircase yelling at us as we stumble up the stairs like toddlers. God is patient with us. For me, I have always been very stubborn and independent. One of my mother's favorite stories about me as a child is that when I learned how to climb steps, the last thing I was going to do was ask for help from my parents. My parents were patient with me as I took my time getting my chubby self up each of those steps. God gives us our independence and allows us to climb each step even though it would be easier just to carry us to the top.

Where we get it wrong is when we fall, we feel like failures. I tried to do this on my own but now I've slipped and fell. Maybe I've even started going back down the steps because I feel discouraged and will never reach the top on my own. God is watching me fail, and do you think He ever tried to help? Do you think He even cares about me because I'm trying my best?

Did you ask for help? At any point as you were climbing and tripped, did you look up towards God or did you immediately look down on yourself and take the blame? God is a good father who cares about his children, and He allows us to live independently. Just like a good parent, when we fall and reach up toward Him is when He picks us up and gets us back on our feet. We have to be brave enough and humble enough to realize that we can NEVER reach the top by ourselves, and we shouldn't want to.

An easy thing to always remember, and remind yourself, is that the theme song playing in hell is Frank Sinatra's song "My Way." (yes it is a wonderful song.)

Make today the courageous day that you reach up to God and ask Him for help. When we ask God for help, it starts with that first step. If we are to get back on track, we must start small. Depending on where we all are on our faith journey, we can start with the same approach. Increase your exposure to God so that you can hear him. This is making the choices that we discussed in the previous segment about where to find God. Listening to Catholic speakers, doing daily readings, taking a moment to pray in the morning, listening to Christian music on your drive to work, and talking to people in your faith community. Let us walk together side by side with God as we take that important first step.

5 Minutes

I guarantee that no matter who you ask, every adult in this country would have at least one thing in common, and that is we are all just way too busy. Well, at least we say we are. When you start adding in jobs, exercise, hobbies, family activities, and commuting, we barely have any time for ourselves. At least that is what we like to think. It makes us feel more accomplished knowing we have a full schedule, but also makes it easier to say no to invitations. The introvert in all of us loves to make an excuse to not commit to plans just so we can stay at home. I'll be honest, even writing this book I always come up with random things on my honey-do list just so I don't feel bad about not taking time to write.

How often do we say no to God when He invites us to learn more about him, and we give the lazy answer of "I'm just too busy?" Now if you truly are too busy for God, then you might want to start looking at what you prioritize in your life. *"If you are too busy to pray ... you are too busy"* (St. Mother Teressa[7])

You might need to cut back on a few things to make room for Him, but for the majority of us, we have plenty of opportunities to invite God into our lives.

---

[7] Teresa, and Matthew Kelly. *Do something beautiful for God: The essential teachings of mother teresa: 365 daily reflections.* North Palm Beach, FL: Blue Sparrow, 2019.

Do you have 5 minutes to give to God? You would be surprised how taking one small action can help you get to know God. Remember, the first step in building this relationship is getting to know Him. Think of it as a spiritual icebreaker.

When people look at others who are devoted to God and can hear Him in their lives, they tend to scoff with doubt that they heard anything. "I've never heard him, so how can you?" We sometimes will jump to conclusions and become judgemental of other people's relationship with God. My first question is, are you inviting God to speak to you in your day-to-day life? The reason that certain people more commonly hear from God is that they continually have His presence around them. They give Him numerous avenues to speak to them. That is when your relationship with Him is growing.

If you want to get to this point in your faith journey, start with 5 minutes to get to know God. 5 minutes of your drive to listen to a new worship song or a hymn. Watch one short video on Youtube every day made by a priest or catholic commentator. Find daily quotes, bible verses, or meditations to get your mind thinking about God. Find a good book on a subject that interests you and read it for a few minutes. We want to start building a habit of keeping God's voice in our lives.

5 minutes isn't the end goal, but the starting line. It is no different if you are exercising and start running on a treadmill. If I tried running today, I don't know if I would make it the whole 5 minutes. Each second would tick by slower than the previous one. It would take all my focus and

determination just to not pass out. If I made an effort every day to run on the treadmill for 5 minutes, soon the 5 minutes would become my warm-up to a long enduring run. The physical and mental challenges in life become difficult only when we lose the ambition to make them a priority.

Taking this same approach to expand your knowledge of God, you will find yourself wanting to learn more, and soon seeing your 5 minutes turn into a half hour, then an hour, and eventually your entire day is filled with God's presence.

It has never been easier to increase our exposure to God. There are thousands of wonderful Catholic books written. Find a topic that fascinates you and look into it. Build your understanding of the church's teachings. If you don't have time to read because your job requires you to drive, then search for some of the numerous Catholic podcasts, or if you have a Catholic radio station in your area, turn that on. Even this book is designed so that every topic can be knocked out in 5-10 minute segments.

The most impactful thing you can do is to find others in your area faith community and be open to having a conversation with them. Whether it's the local priest, a catechist, or a neighbor you trust, find someone you can discuss your questions, doubts, and what confuses you. Find groups like the Council of Catholic Women, Knights of Columbus, or other groups in your parish where parishioners gather outside of their weekly Sunday commitment. If you are fully committed to making this change in your life, find someone else to do it with you. This could be a spouse, friend, or neighbor that you hold each other accountable. It gives you someone that you can go to when your motivation is running low. When I started to have my big awakening in my own faith life, it started with my wife and I reading a book every night after supper. What started as 10 minutes of reading has turned into reading daily quotes from saints, daily bible readings, prayers, and reflection. Eventually, it becomes an important part of your day that you don't want to miss. If you want God to speak to you, give Him avenues, and people to speak through.

It is never too late to start your spiritual development, but you must take that first step. Let us look at a parable from the Gospel of Matthew.

> *For the kingdom of Heaven is like a landowner who went out early in the morning to hire labourers for his vineyard. After agreeing with the labourers for the usual daily wage, he sent them into the vineyard. When he went out about nine o'clock, he saw others standing idle in the market-place; and he said to them, "You also go into the vineyard, and I will pay you whatever is right." So they went. When he went out again about noon and about three o'clock, he did the same. And about five o'clock he went out and found others standing around; and he said to them, "Why are you standing here idle all day?" They said to him, "Because no one has hired us." He said to them, "You also go into the vineyard." When evening came, the owner of the vineyard said to his manager, "Call the labourers and give them their pay, beginning with the last and going to the first." When those hired about five o'clock came, each of them received the usual daily wage. Now when*

the first came, they thought they would receive more; but each of them also received the usual daily wage. And when they received it, they grumbled against the landowner, saying, "These last worked only one hour, and you have made them equal to us who have borne the burden of the day and the scorching heat." But he replied to one of them, "Friend, I am doing you no wrong; did you not agree with me for the usual daily wage? Take what belongs to you and go; I choose to give to this last the same as I give to you. Am I not allowed to do what I choose with what belongs to me? Or are you envious because I am generous? So the last will be first and the first will be last.

Matthew 20:1-16

Remember that our God is generous. He wants to see all of His children come home and have a relationship with us all. He doesn't care if we are born into His church, if we discover Him after our marriage, or if we stumble upon His teachings in our old age. We are all promised the same reward. Now for those baptized into the faith and spending their whole life trying to be perfect, that might not seem fair. If others get to spend their whole lives in sin, and suddenly get saved at the last moment, don't let your jealousy get the better of you. Let us all rejoice in one another who shares the love for our Lord.

So do you have 5 minutes to spare? Find something that interests you, and plant that seed. Allow God to nourish your soul and through His love, your spirit will begin to flourish and take shape. Do not hesitate.

Reading the Bible

It has never been easier to learn and understand the word of God. I don't think this is too outlandish of a statement to make when you look at all of our resources provided to help us read it. I'm not just talking about apps and being able to google any verse in an instance, but the fact that we have more scholars than ever breaking down the bible word by word. Translations are becoming more accurate than ever, and we are seeing a deeper commitment by the population to understand it.

To understand the importance and significance of the Bible, we need to understand what the Bible is. Although we look at the Bible as a singular book, it's more accurately described as a library. Within the Bible, there are 73 different books. These books were written by numerous authors, over 1,500 years, and written in three different languages (Hebrew, Aramaic, and Greek).

When the Catholic Church started its mission to spread the teachings of Christ after Pentecost, the apostles didn't have a canonized New Testament to hand out but went from town to town to teach. This was how the church was started and why the church has an emphasis on sacred tradition. When Jesus taught, He instructed them to DO, not to write. Over the next 60 years, after Christ's resurrection, the Apostles would finish their writings, and the scriptural texts would spread throughout the young church.

The biggest challenge of the early church was staying consistent as this underground church began to spread. Part of the problem was that not all of the works being taught were inspired by God. There were numerous other gospels and apostolic books that were used in different areas of the church but would be found to be unreliable teachings. (Apocalypse of Peter, the gospel of James, etc)

The first time the church finally had a canonized bible with all the books compiled into one wasn't until the year 393, after the council of Hippo. For over 360 years, the church was held together by the sacred traditions passed down by Jesus Christ and continued by apostolic succession. Scripture was already an important part of the Catholic Mass, but certain sections of the church would prioritize certain apostles, and books over others. The canonization of the Bible allowed the Catholic Church to teach sacred scripture consistently as the young church continued to spread to every corner of the globe.

The biggest reason that the Bible has never been easier to learn than it is today is as simple as you can read it on your own. The earliest Christians could not read or write. Even some of the Apostles most likely could not read or write when they first met Jesus. So how did the first Christians learn scripture? Through the Mass. Anyone that has attended a Catholic Mass knows that the majority of the Mass is what we call the Liturgy of the Word. This is composed of a reading from the Old Testament, singing of a Psalm, a New Testament reading, and then a Gospel reading. After all the scripture is read, the priest gives his homily, or his teaching of the scripture. Without the Mass, the earliest Christians would have never learned the word of God. Now even if they could read, it would be incredibly unlikely that they would be sitting at home reading the Gospels considering that everything had to be handwritten. It would have cost a fortune to privately own a copy. Fast forward 2,000 years, the bible is printed everywhere, it's on our phones, children's Bibles are available with colorful pictures, and we can listen to someone else read it to us, and break down what we just read. Shout out to Fr. Mike Schmitz.[8] Even today in America we still have roughly 12% of the population who is illiterate. So, how can we ensure that everyone knows what's in the Bible?

      Well, let's go back to the church's original solution. Go to Mass. You see even 2,000 years later, the Catholic church is on a three-year cycle. Meaning that over 3 years, roughly 80% of the Bible will be read through daily Mass. When I grew up, I understood what the scripture taught, and I knew the stories, but where they occurred and in what order, I could never have told you. I wasn't going to win any Bible Bowls or outsmart anyone with my Bible knowledge, but that never meant I was dumb or ignorant about my faith. It is as if I was giving directions to a friend's house. I couldn't tell you the exact address, but I know how to get there by certain landmarks and from my experience of traveling there.

---

[8] Schmitz, Mike, Jeff Cavins, and Lavinia Spirito. *The Bible in a year companion*. West Chester, PA: Ascension, 2022.

So if the Mass reads us the Bible, then why read it at home? Let's look at the common criticisms of modern Catholics, and let's see if this sounds familiar. If we only rely on the Mass and neglect the resources to learn about God, then we assume that one hour on Sunday is good enough. How much deeper would our knowledge of God be if we committed ourselves to meditating every day on His Word? What's beautiful about the Bible is God uses it to speak to you today. It doesn't matter how many times you've heard the stories, or sung the Psalms, because whatever point you are at in life, and whatever challenges you are facing, that scripture will hit you differently.

When my wife started her RCIA program to convert to the Catholic church, I was her sponsor, and there were a few other married couples in the program as well. The Deacon running the program commented about the Protestant in the relationship most likely knew the Bible more fluently than the Catholic spouse. At first, this statement made me proud and embarrassed thinking "Absolutely not." The more I thought about it, just because I was the sponsor didn't mean I had all the answers. Neither my wife nor I had ever really sat down to read the Bible in our spare time. It was a beautiful way to start off our marriage by identifying that this was an area in which we could grow together. Now every night after supper, we read the Bible, or other saintly books.

As Catholics, we should never let our lack of knowing the Bible be acceptable, or become a badge of honor. Remember that the Bible is your history. When you read the *Acts of the Apostles*, you are looking at the first steps of your church after the incredible first Pentecost. Learn who you are through scripture. My favorite historical quote comes from President John Quincy Adams when he said, "Who we are is who we were."[9] We are all Adam and Eve, the Israelites wandering through the desert, or Peter denying Christ.

Before, I called the Bible a library. We sometimes take for granted how beautifully the Bible is laid out. Ancient stories that are over 3,500 years old, written in three different languages, written by Kings, prophets, and fishermen. All come together to form one beautiful love story. Yes, the Bible is the greatest love story ever written. The reason that I can confidently say that, is because it perfectly lays out how patient God is with us. Many will read the Old Testament and think that there is no way that this is the same God as in the New Testament and that when they see God throughout that, He is changing. God never changes.

When we think of God we have to remember that God lives outside of time and space. He is never the perfect God of this age, but the perfect God for all ages. He knows when we are going to turn from Him and He knows what's best for us. God knew every time in the Old Testament when His chosen people were going to disobey Him and fall into temptation. It wasn't God who changed throughout the Bible, but His people. As His people changed so did His approach, and eventually, a new covenant was formed.

Imagine how much differently we act in America in just over 100 years. In the same century, America went from prohibiting alcohol to legalizing marijuana. Over time people continuously change based on their desires, goals, and

---

[9] Spielberg, Steven. 1997. *Amistad*. United States: DreamWorks Distribution.

whatever is trending. Now imagine the changes that happened over 1,500 years, and think of where we are today 2,000 years later.

Through all the changes God stayed true to His chosen people. The Old Testament is filled with stories of the chosen people in a roller coaster relationship with God, with each generation getting closer or farther away. Yet, God stayed true to His promise and you can hear Him saying, "I will wait." His love was so great that He sent His only son to fulfill all the promises of the Old Testament and die for our sins. Leaving us with the tools to love and serve our neighbor and build a better world.

Find a Bible, or download the app on your phone, and allow God to speak to you through His word. Soon you will hear Him say, "I love you!".

Personal Relationship with God

When I first met my wife, we were at a mutual friend's wedding, but I didn't notice her until much later in the evening when the dance started. Now, I didn't plan on staying too late, because I had to work the next morning, and just wasn't feeling like drinking and dancing. That all changed when I saw this gorgeous woman dancing to a Meatloaf song. Everything changed. I know it's not super romantic but for context, Meatloaf is one of my father's favorite singers and all of us kids grew up to love the 8-9 minute song. When I saw this beautiful woman who actually knew who Meatloaf was, I knew I had to talk to her.

All of my plans had changed and I was now focused on talking to her. I was genuinely a shy and awkward guy, but I was able to muster up enough courage to ask her to dance. Luckily she said yes. I couldn't tell you what song we were dancing to because I knew I only had a few minutes to talk with her. Of course, we introduced ourselves, talked about our families, and made a few attempts at jokes. When the dancing stopped I had the bare minimum of understanding who this gal was. If I was going to be able to continue the conversation then maybe I would have a chance.

Our paths didn't cross again until the end of the night when I was ready to leave. I asked her for her number and once again was lucky enough to get it. The following day, the conversation picked up again. We continued with the usual small talk to get to know each other and after the first few weeks, those short messages turned into borderline novels as we started getting deeper into the conversation. Texting was fine, but it had gotten to the point where we needed to see each other again. Setting up dates wasn't always the easiest because we lived an hour and a half apart, but found a few ways to make it work.

Our first "date" was a weekend in Brooking SD where we tailgated with my family and her friends and then went to the football game. Now, usually, I am laser focused when my Jackrabbits are playing football and my dad and I are talking throughout the whole game, but not this game. My whole focus was on this girl (Jacks won 38-3 so didn't miss much).

We talked through the whole game which had become background noise. Hours and hours we talked and that night we never left each other's sides. We walked around town talking and being goofy. Stayed up until almost 2 in the morning just enjoying each other's time. That personal experience was the spark that led to our marriage, and the start of our family.

It is funny how crucial dates are to a relationship. Growing up in a small town, the common first date experience was a movie because there really wasn't much else to do. How impractical is going to a movie when you can't see your date, there's no talking, and your attention is intentionally directed at something else? Dates don't have to be complicated, it's just two people making the effort to spend time with each other. Whether it's picnics, dinner, or even hitting up a bowling alley. It's the effort that matters.

Since this isn't a book about dating, I must ask the question, how do we "date" God? Weird question isn't it, but it's something we need to ask ourselves. Up to this point, we have been introduced to God, and we've started giving Him at least 5 minutes a day. We have opened up His book and are deepening our understanding of who He is, but we still haven't established a more personal relationship. So we need to make the effort to "date" God.

This opportunity is available every single day in the Catholic Church when Mass is being held. For many, if it is their first experience participating in a Catholic Mass, it is going to be a sensory overload. You don't know what to say, the terminology sounds like the priest is speaking a different language (which he actually is), and you feel left out when everyone else knows how to properly kneel, sit, and stand. You may be visually mesmerized by all the incredible artwork, the beautiful vestments, and even the unique smells of the church. When you walk out, you might even think to yourself "I'm not sure what was even going on." Trust me, even many Catholics may become numb to the elements of the church and the details of the Catholic Mass. Remember, we are trying to break the sleepwalking through our faith for us cradle Catholics.

Whether you have gone to hundreds of Masses before or have never stepped foot into a Catholic church, we need to start putting in the effort of going to Mass every week. If we are truly committed to building a relationship with God, we need to spend time with Him in His house. I mean you don't stop dating your spouse after you get married, do you?

The more we attend Mass, the more scripture comes alive. Each year we go through different seasons of the church and it allows us to walk as a community with Christ through the Old Testament and His ministry. You can't get that experience by attending Mass twice a year or dusting off your Bible every few months. The Catholic Mass is a beautiful commitment to God, and to better ourselves.

For any relationship to work, both individuals have to be willing to give 100%. God is present in every Catholic Church around the world and can be visited every day through Mass. There is no doubt how much He loves every one of us and wants a more personal relationship with us. Let us now walk through the church year and how we can put in the effort of "dating" God. Are you ready to give your 100%?

Advent and Christmas

HAPPY NEW YEAR! This is a guaranteed joke that every Catholic priest will say after Thanksgiving when the new church year starts. As mentioned before, the Catholic Church has a set liturgical calendar that works on a three-year cycle. Within each year, the church celebrates different seasons. The majority of the year is called ordinary time where we get the bulk of Jesus's teachings throughout His ministry. The special seasons include Advent, Christmas, Lent, and Easter throughout the year. Each one with its own set of teachings and traditions. A common practice in the Catholic Church is to live out our faith in the Mass.

The Church year begins with the season of Advent which is the four weeks between Thanksgiving and Christmas. Advent is the season of preparation. As we enter this season, we remember our past but look forward to the future. This four-week season is split up into two main focus points. During the first two weeks, we reflect on the people of Israel anticipating the coming of the Messiah. For centuries, the people of Israel listened to the words of the prophets and anticipated the arrival of their savior. This was fulfilled 2,000 years ago with the birth of Jesus Christ.

If we are committed to building a personal relationship with God and committing ourselves to Him, we need to get to know who He is and where He comes from.

During the Advent season, we get introduced to the family of Jesus, also known as the Holy Family.

Front and center, of course, is His mother, Mary. Mary was a young Jewish woman who was filled with the grace of God and lived a sinless life. Mary's devotion to God was on full display when the Angel Gabriel revealed to Mary that she would bear the Son of God.

> *The angel said to her, 'Do not be afraid, Mary, for you have found favor with God. And now, you will conceive in your womb and bear a son, and you will name him Jesus. Then Mary said, 'Here am I, the servant of the Lord; let it be with me according to your word.'*
>
> *Luke 1:30-31, 38*

The example that Mary shows us is simple yet challenging. God has a plan for all of us, but not always what we desire. Throughout our lives, we focus on what we want and set goals based on a desire for fame, money, or personal accomplishment. None of those things are bad, but if we feel that God is calling us to serve in a different field, or wants to take our lives in a new direction, we aren't always eager to make those changes.

Sometimes we could be asking God for a change or opportunity, and still not be willing to say yes. When I was in college, I was attending Mass and was going through my usual round of prayers. "Feed the hungry, shelter the homeless, and defend the defenseless". On this specific Sunday, I started to change up my prayers and asked God to give me the opportunity to answer these prayers. "Lord help me feed the hungry, help me shelter the homeless, and help me defend the defenseless." Trust me when I say to you that God wasted no time answering that prayer. Later in the Mass, they were reading the announcements and wouldn't you know it, they were looking for volunteers to help chaperon a trip to a local homeless shelter to serve food. There are certainly times that God whispers but this was Him screaming at me with a big flashing sign.

So of course I signed up right? Well, you see even though I had asked for this opportunity as soon as it was presented to me, my selfish nature stepped in. I immediately started to make excuses as to why I couldn't make that date work, and just too busy, but I'm sure I'll sign up next time though. It's one thing to say the right thing when we are praying, but are we willing to say yes when God calls us? Something as simple as volunteering an afternoon is easy for us to ignore, or find a way around. So what was the end result of rejecting God? My computer crashed. I lost everything on it and had to go buy a new one. Great way to end freshman year.

Now could you imagine if you were asked to raise a child? How about the Son of God? Our immediate thought would be that we aren't worthy, we wouldn't be good enough parents, or maybe we just didn't want to be parents. Yet, when a young, teenage, Jewish girl was approached with the same situation without hesitation, she responded with a confident, "Yes."

Mary has been given many titles after her assumption into Heaven. Blessed Virgin, Our Lady, Mother of God, and Queen of Heaven, to name a few. One of the titles given to

Mary is the "New Eve". This is about, of course, the first woman that God created. Eve was created for Adam, and as he was at his creation, free from sin. As we know, Adam and Eve fell to temptation from the serpent and fell into a life of sin. This sin is something that all mankind carries with them to this day except for one. Mary was Immaculately conceived and was free from sin at her birth and maintained a sinless life. By God's design, Mary was created to be the New Eve, of a new creation, where there will be a sinless kingdom which we commonly call Heaven.

If Mary is Eve, then who is Adam? Well, if we look back at Genesis, Eve was created from Adam, for Adam. In the New Testament, Mary was created by the Father, for the Son. A perfect woman, free from sin, blessed to carry the Son of God. A woman professed to squash the serpent's head and give birth to a new covenant.

Remember, the Bible is split up into two parts. The Old and New Testaments. Another way to look at this is the old and new covenants. So what is the old covenant? During the Old Testament, we see God's covenant begin with Abraham and continue with David. God promises vast lines of descendants, land, and protection as long as they stay faithful to God. Throughout the Old Testament, we get introduced to new laws for this covenant and God's chosen people. Although the chosen people aren't always faithful and fall in and out of love with the Father, God stays loyal to His chosen people, but not without a few consequences along the way. During their reign in Israel, the Jewish people found themselves being conquered and under foreign leadership. Eventually, the Romans took control. God promised that one day He would send a savior to free the Jewish people. Jesus is the fulfillment of the old covenant, and that is why the New Testament begins with His birth.

The other time we hear the term covenant, in scripture, is when we hear about the Ark of the Covenant. If you have ever watched Indiana Jones, your ears might have perked up a bit. The Ark of the Covenant was the vessel that held the Ten Commandments, as well as Aaron's staff, and manna. Each item individually has incredible meaning. The Ten Commandments represent the Law of God, Aaron's staff was a sign of his priestly role, and manna was the bread from Heaven.

Once again, we bestow another title for Mary as we call her the New Ark of the Covenant. Right off the bat, we identify that Mary conceived and carried Jesus in her womb. Jesus, as we know, is the fulfillment of the old covenant. Within her womb, Mary contained the New Law, the new high priest, and the everlasting bread from Heaven. She was guarded and protected by angels, and no earthly human could do her harm. She was truly elevated above all women.

A woman clothed with the sun, with the moon under her feet, and on her head a crown of twelve stars.

Revelation 12:1

Even with Mary's elevated status and the protection of all the angels, God didn't expect Mary to raise Jesus by herself. For His son must be raised by both a mother and a father. God made a covenant with David about the future of His Kingdom.

> *When your days are fulfilled and you lie down with your ancestors, I will raise up your offspring after you, who shall come forth from your body, and I will establish his kingdom. He shall build a house for my name, and I will establish the throne of his kingdom forever. I will be a father to him, and he shall be a son to me.*
>
> *2 Samuel 7:12-14*

By God's great design, Mary was already engaged to a man named Joseph, who was a descendant of David. Now, when we read the nativity story, it is much more common for us to relate to Joseph. Joseph was a simple, just, righteous, and hard-working carpenter, but didn't see himself as worthy to raise the Son of God. He initially intended to step away quietly for the safety and protection of Mary.

David felt similarly when in the presence of the Ark of the Covenant. Under David's reign, Jerusalem was named the capital of Israel, and he believed that it was the rightful location of the Ark of the Covenant. As David's men carted the Ark from the house of Abinadab, a man named Uzzah, touched the ark when the oxen shook it. Touching the Ark was forbidden and he was struck down by God. David started to fear the Lord after this event.

> *How can the ark of the Lord come into my care? So David was unwilling to take the ark of the Lord into his care in the city of David.*
>
> 2 Samuel 6:9-10

This fear led David to leave the Ark in the home of Obed-edom for three months. The household of Obed-edom was blessed by the Lord because of the Ark's presence. When David heard of this blessing, he had a change of heart and proceeded to rally his men to finish the journey to Jerusalem. As the Ark was carried into the city, it was led by its King.

> *David danced before the Lord with all his might ... David and all the house of Israel brought up the ark of the Lord with shouting, and with the sound of trumpets.*
>
> 2 Samuel 6:14-15

Joseph's heart was troubled by the news of Mary's pregnancy. He feared that she would be exposed to public disgrace, and potentially be stoned to death. Before Joseph took action, an Angel of God appeared to him in a dream and said to him,

> *Joseph, son of David, do not be afraid to take Mary as your wife, for the child conceived in her is from the Holy Spirit. She will bear a son, and you are to name him Jesus, for he will save his people from their sins.*

Matthew 1:20-21

Joseph then took Mary to be his wife, and raised Jesus as his son. Although Joseph doesn't say a single word in the Bible, that doesn't mean that his role was small. Even though Joseph was a sinner, just like us, he was the one who held Jesus when he cried as a baby and picked Him up when he fell. It was also Joseph who raised Jesus to be the man he became. How to work, laugh, love, and pray.

A father's role is to set an example for his children. Jesus followed in Joseph's footsteps as a child. At the crucifixion, he gave his parents to us for spiritual guidance. Not only did Mary become our mother, but Joseph also became our spiritual father. Let us pray that we can be inspired by Joseph until the day of our death, and even at the hour of our death, follow his example. When Joseph's final hour came, he was in the presence of Jesus and Mary to finish his journey. This is why we ask Mary to pray for us at the hour of our death when we say the Hail Mary.

As we celebrate the season of Advent, we are filled with anticipation and excitement, like a new mother carrying her child in the womb. Awaiting the arrival of Jesus, and preparing to make sure that everything is ready for the newborn baby. Advent isn't a season only for remembering the past but for our preparation. This is why the final two weeks are in place for us to prepare for the second coming.

> *In my Father's house there are many dwelling places. If it were not so, would I have told you that I go to prepare a place for you? And if I go and prepare a place*

for you, I will come again and will take you to myself, so that where I am, there you may also be.

John 14:2-3

As Catholics, we recognize that through Christ's death, resurrection, and ascension into Heaven, He will soon be returning to bring us to His kingdom. We begin our year with the self-reflection of our hearts and if we are ready for the second coming of Christ, for we do not know the day nor the hour.

    It's ok to feel like you may never be truly prepared. We alone are not worthy to be received into God's kingdom, but through His grace, we will be received. As my wife and I anticipated the birth of our first child, the same doubt crept into our minds. Through that nine months before becoming parents, we made sure that we had clothes, bottles, diapers, toys, books, and all the gadgets to make raising a child simpler (if that's even possible). It was also important that we prepared our hearts and our minds. We didn't know what kind of parents we were going to be or how to even begin to prepare for this endeavor. We both came from different backgrounds and were exposed to different parenting styles. How do we even begin to prepare? Well, it's all about communication. For my wife and I to be good parents, we need to be on the same page on how we want to raise our daughter. What values do we share, what rules will be in place, and we must make every decision together. If we aren't on the same page it will lead to confusion, arguing, and stress on our daughter. At the end of the day, it is our shared love for each other and the love we have for our daughter, that we knew we were prepared for her arrival.

There is no spiritual checklist for the second coming so it's not as easy as reading a book, making a list, and checking the boxes to ensure your spot in Heaven. If we want to be prepared it is through that same love that God has for us. We must look at ourselves and think, "Do I love God?" "Am I willing to do anything for him?" "Am I committed to serving Him and His church?"

Advent is the perfect way to begin our year as we proclaim our commitment to God and our journey to loving Him fully. We may never truly be prepared for His arrival, but prepare your heart and have faith as you walk along the path He lays before you.

When we finally get to Christmas, our longing has been fulfilled with the birth of Christ. We are also reminded of the humble beginning of His birth. To be born in a manger. His whole life, He was poor and His parents had to work for everything they had. His father showed Him how to earn an honest living with the skill of His hands. He learned how to humble Himself before the Lord in prayer. Throughout His ministry, He served all those who longed to hear His teaching and to be healed by Him, but it was their faith that saved them. All leading to Him humbly dying on the cross.

Yet not what I want but what you want

Matthew 26:39

Lent

    If Advent is the beginning of the New Year, then Lent is when we start our New Year resolution. Many Catholics probably look at the season of Lent as nothing more than a built-in diet plan. I mean, all you have to do is give up pop, and candy for forty days, no meat on Fridays if you can remember, and try your best to fast. That's all, right? Of course not. You see Lent is a perfect example of the more you put in, the more you get out. Similar to Advent, it is a season of preparation and if we don't take it seriously, then we won't reach our goal.

    What are we preparing for? We are preparing for Jesus. More specifically, we are preparing for His second coming, just like we are at the end of Advent. After the season of Lent, we enter into the Easter season which begins with the Resurrection. That is what we are preparing our souls for. The problem with thinking that Lent is a Catholic diet plan is that it is focusing on the wrong thing. Lent isn't a season about the body but about the soul. The whole season of Lent is a reminder that our bodies are temporary and that it is our souls that live on forever.

    When we enter into the season of Lent, we begin with Ash Wednesday. Ash Wednesday is a beautiful Mass that is filled with so much incredible imagery and tradition. To begin, let us start with the motto of Ash Wednesday "We are dust and to dust we shall return." Kind of morbid isn't it? If we miss interpret it, we could make it seem that we are meaningless and that we don't matter in the grand scheme of things. Now is this really what God is trying to tell us? The answer is of course not. This is a reminder of our creation and a reminder of our imminent death. Let us look back at the creation of man laid out in Genesis.

> *Then the Lord God formed man from the dust of the ground, and breathed into his nostrils the breath of life; and the man became a living being.*
>
> *Genesis 2:7*

Through the power of God, He created us in His image, from the Earth, but it is through us that we welcomed death into the world. After the first sin, God punished Adam and Eve.

> *By the sweat of your face you shall eat bread until you return to the ground for out of it you were taken; you are dust and to dust you shall return.*
>
> *Genesis 3:19*

Death is our reward for a life of sin. This isn't breaking news because we all know that we will all die someday. Although death is a guarantee, that doesn't mean that death is something to fear. As Christ will show us after His death, we can be assured that there is victory over death, where we can overcome our sins and be joined with the Father in paradise.

So why Ashes? Throughout the Old Testament, we consistently see the use of ashes and dust being used as a sign of mourning or grief. To be even more specific, the Ashes are placed on their heads when they are in this state. When Joshua was leading the Israelites and they broke their faith in God and the hearts of the people failed, he entered a state of grieving.

> *Then Joshua tore his clothes, and fell to the ground on his face before the ark of the Lord until the evening, he and the elders of Israel; and they put dust on their heads.*
>
> *Joshua 7:6*

On Ash Wednesday, we are mourning our sins, and our continued failure to give God our hearts fully. We are reminded of how much we have failed him, and through our sins, we place the ashes on our heads. Although we take responsibility for our sins we are reminded that we are a community of sinners. Remember, that the Catholic Church isn't a church only for saints, but a church full of sinners trying to become saints. As a community, we approach the altar with heavy hearts and mourn for our conversions. Together, we look forward to when we rise from the Ashes through the grace of God.

> *The Spirit of the Lord God is upon me, because the Lord has anointed me; he has sent me to bring good news to the oppressed, to bind up the broken hearted, ... to*

proclaim the year of the Lord's favor and the day of vengeance of our God; to comfort all who mourn; to provide for those who mourn in Zion to give them a garland instead of ashes, the oil of gladness instead of mourning, the mantle of praise instead of a faint spirit.

Isaiah 61:1-3

Through the sacrifice of Jesus and our commitment to bettering ourselves, sin doesn't have the final word. We can never live sinless lives, but as long as our love for Jesus is strong, and our perseverance to overcome our sins is continuous, we can find victory over sin. We find that victory through our death. All death results in sadness, and heartbreak, but also should be celebrated. After our death, our bodies return to the earth to become dust, and from the dust, we rise with Christ to be welcomed into the kingdom He has prepared for us. To live in unison with Him for eternity.

To obtain this victory, we must continue our daily battle with sin, and can't become complacent. We all face different challenges and certainly have had our share of victories in the past. Although we relish in our ability to conquer sin, we must be vigilant to avoid new sins and seek to become saintly.

For us to truly embrace this mindset, we first need to look to our local priests. For starters, the priest is the spiritual father in our church and community. Although the domestic church begins in the home from the parent's teachings, the local priest guides the faith community as one body. Remember our local priest is in a direct, and unbroken, line to St. Peter and Jesus. The priests guide us through our lives with their teachings and service to us.

One thing we might take for granted is how our priests dress. Now I'm not talking about the beautiful vestments that they wear while celebrating the Mass, but the black attire they wear day in and day out. Now just like everything in the church even the priestly clothing has a specific meaning and can teach us a lesson. The reason that priests wear black is because it represents the death of self.[10] A life devoted to the service of others, and not self-recognition and glory. The simplicity of wearing black represents a life of modesty and reminds us that the material goods of this world don't hold any value. The color black also has historical significance in mourning or a time of penance. Penance in the Catholic Church is a sign of healing and forgiveness. Living a life of penance, it is the priestly mission to live a life of healing, forgiveness, and repentance. When we are in a community, we should take time to get to know our priests and understand what their lives are.

One of the biggest misconceptions about the lives of priests is that they have a lot of free time when they aren't celebrating Mass. This couldn't be farther from the truth. Depending on the location of a priest, they are certainly involved in the numerous councils that make a church function, education programs, and potentially helping run a school if they have one. Classes to prepare the parishioners for Baptism, Reconciliation, first communion, Confirmation,

---

[10] Hoerner, Michael. "Hey, Father! Why Do Priests Wear Black?" NEW FLAG APPROVED JPEG, September 29, 2019. ct.dio.org

and Matrimony. The priest offers times of adoration and times for Reconciliation. Helping families with funerals after losing a loved one. Visits to homebound parishioners to receive Communion and final blessings. Emergency trips to hospitals to pray for the souls of people in critical states, as well as, emergency Baptism, Confirmations, and anointing for newborn infants in critical condition. This doesn't mention the hours of prayer they are devoted to doing, offering Mass daily, and living a life of additional service leading parishioners to serve the poor and needy. I encourage anyone who wants to gain respect for your local priest, to sit down and talk with them about their daily routine, or watch some of the remarkable videos on youtube about a day or a week in the life of a priest.

  We aren't all called to be priests or nuns, but to live out the vocations we are called to. Even if we own a business, are nurses, or are insurance agents, we all are called to follow the priestly example of the death of self or to put it in simpler terms to live a selfless life. The lenten season helps us get closer to attaining this goal, but what does that even look like? This gets to the misconception of the "Catholic diet plan". When Lent begins, we give up something, we fast on Ash Wednesday and every Friday, and we abstain from meat, and alcohol on Fridays. This isn't designed to be a punishment but an exercise. When we give up a guilty pleasure like alcohol, snacking, sweets, or anything else, we are trying to find something that we enjoy and frequently use. It allows us to say "no" to our desires and temptations. Although it's not a sin to have a drink, getting drunk is. How often do we overindulge in drinking and then find ourselves not fit enough to attend Sunday Mass? Do we ever sit down and eat a whole bag of potato chips in one sitting, but neglect to give $5 to the special collection for the food shelf? You see when we look at the sins we most commonly commit, it tends to be physical sins. Sins of greed, jealousy, power, gluttony, and adultery. When we live selfish lives and never say no to ourselves, our desire is always to have more. So a small sin continuously grows into something greater. It will keep growing until you stand up and say, "NO!" That is why we exercise our bodies and our minds during Lent to allow us to start fighting off temptations. It's hard to give up things we enjoy, but we need to acknowledge that just because it makes us happy, doesn't mean it's good. Even if it's a sin in privacy, it is still harming others in your life because it alters the person you are becoming.

  When we are faced with temptation, we must not give up. Just because you are tempted to do something or an unclean thought runs through your head, that doesn't mean you have sinned. Temptation is the devil's way of luring us into sin, but in itself, isn't a sinful act. Remember, even Jesus was tempted. The whole season of Lent is based on the experience that Christ had in the wilderness. For forty days and forty nights, Christ fasted and was famished. His Body would have become weaker from suffering through the scorching heat, while His mind would become clouded. He was at His most vulnerable state and that's when the devil came. Looking at His hunger, the devil tempted Jesus to break His fast by turning stones into bread, when he found himself unsuccessful, he wanted Christ to test God by throwing himself off the temple. When Jesus refused to fall into temptation the devil showed Him all the kingdoms of the world and their riches *(Matt 4:1-11)*. Every time Jesus refused to fall into temptation and stayed loyal to God. With each temptation, the devil tried to satisfy His needs, create doubt about God, and tempt Him with power and money. When we face our temptations, it's the same approach. The devil tempts us with physical and earthly desires. To satisfy our hunger, lust, and personal emptiness. He tempts us with greed through money, power, and possessions. When it's all said and done, he lets doubt creep into our minds if we need God in our lives, or even if He exists. He inflates our minds to believe that everything we accomplish was done on our own.

We aren't always going to have the perfect answer when we fall into temptation and sin. It happens and it will continue to happen. That is why God gave us the gift of Reconciliation. When we sin, it is normal for us to repent of these sins and regret committing them. This is a gift given to us from Christ through His apostles.

> *'Peace be with you. As the Father has sent me, so I send you.' When he had said this, he breathed on them and said to them, 'Receive the Holy Spirit. If you forgive the sins of any, they are forgiven them; if you retain the sins of any, they are retained.'*
>
> John 20:21-22

This blessing has been passed down through the apostles to every priest over the last 2,000 years. Your local priest received this same blessing when he was ordained. When we repent and confess our sins to our local priest, we have confidence that we are confessing them to Christ through the priest. Whenever you receive this sacrament, you can feel the freeing relief of sin being lifted off your shoulders. When my wife received it for the first time, the experience filled her body with relief, and out came tears. Happy tears of course.

Don't be discouraged if you continue to fall in and out of sin. We all have sins that are harder to overcome than others. We will never be perfect, but that doesn't mean we shouldn't strive to be. As we continue going through this faith journey together, we are growing stronger, but that's not without blemish. As we grow stronger and we conquer sin, we know that we never do it alone. It is easy for us to feel prideful when we overcome sin. It is through the strength and grace of God that we can overcome sin. It is through Him that all things are possible. It is through Him that we will rise on the last day.

Does God Know You?

One of the greatest blessings we have in our church is all the beautiful artwork that fills it. From towering windows to beautifully etched stations and powerful statues, the beauties of St. Mary's are breathtaking.

When we look at each window, it is easy to take for granted the amount of detail that went into making them.

From the smallest symbol, to the perfect moment to capture an entire story from the bible, or which saints will inspire our crowds. Every detail was designed for a reason and has a purpose. Their purpose is to show God's beauty and to tell God's story.

Sadly over time we take them for granted and forget about them. Eventually, they become "Saint what's his name", and "Mr. Important for some reason." They simply become a general background.

When we visit the church at night and the lights are turned off, and the sun has set, what do we see? We see that all the beautiful colors have faded to black. Without light, the windows can't serve their purpose. It is at this moment that the windows turn into mirrors, showing us what we look like when we turn off God's light.

Just like the windows, God made every single one of us with so much detail, and to be beautiful images of himself. Each one is unique with the purpose of sharing God's story for all who see it, but we need the light. The windows should be a reminder to us every Sunday, as we watch the morning sunshine through them, that we need the light of God to shine through us all to brighten up the world. It is then that we can fulfill the purpose of who God created us to be.

Yet, it seems like being unique is harder every day. Today, everyone is concerned about going viral, being trendy, and sticking with whatever is popular. As we talked about earlier, the public popularity contest doesn't invite God into the conversation. Popular culture is intentionally driving a wedge between you and God by design. Remember, the devil invites you in with physical desires, power, money, and fame.

As we grow up, we lose the imaginative youthfulness that makes us unique just to trade it in for herd mentality.

We change our passions, our looks, and habits to conform ourselves to be just like everyone else. We are told that being unique isn't popular, or that you will be made fun of for being different, but God made us to be different. Just like the stained glass windows, we were all made for a purpose by God's grand design.

Remember we were all made in His image and likeness, but what does that even mean? My favorite way of explaining this came from a video I stumbled upon by Pastor Michael Todd.[11] The algorithm must have been broken that day because it actually suggested something helpful and enlightening. What Pastor Todd focused on is the relationship a glove has with a hand. What does the glove look like? It has fingers like a hand and is shaped like a hand. It has been created by the hand in its image and likeness, but if it is not in unison with the hand then it is not fulfilling its purpose. Without the hand, others may use it as a rag, and it'll be abused, or broken. If it's not with the hand, it could be lost or thrown away without fulfilling its purpose. It's not until the hand fills the glove that it fulfills its purpose.

When we don't fulfill our purpose and don't have God's light shining through us, the world becomes darker and colder. Like the dark months of winter, life is shut away into hibernation, covered up by the cold snow, and the days are filled with darkness. It becomes a time of sadness, isolation,

---

[11] Todd, Michael. "You Were Created For God." Lecture, September 19, 2020.

and loneliness. When we can't see the light, we start to believe that there is no God and that there is no light. I assure you, even in the darkest times, that light lives in us all. It is up to us to allow that light to shine through us. If we allow God's light to shine, we will show everyone the beauty that God created us to be. We can shine light into the world to show everyone there is hope, love, and beauty through God. A light that will warm the hearts of the lost, and spring new life into this cold, dark world.

So far in this faith journey, we have been making an effort in getting to know God. We have read His word, listened to His people, and followed His servants. We have been welcomed into His house and we are beginning to understand who He is. His light is kindling inside us, but does God know us? Let's listen to a parable taught by Jesus to help answer this question.

> *"Then the kingdom of Heaven will be like this. Ten bridesmaids took their lamps and went to meet the bridegroom. Five of them were foolish, and five were wise. When the foolish took their lamps, they took no oil with them, but the wise took flasks of oil with their lamps. As the bridegroom was delayed, all of them became drowsy and slept. But at midnight there was a shout, 'Look! Here is the bridegroom! Come out to meet him.' Then all those bridesmaids got up and trimmed their lamps. The foolish said to the wise, 'Give us some of your oil, for our lamps are going out.' But the wise replied, 'No! there will not be enough for you and for us; you had better go to the dealers and buy some for*

yourselves.' And while they went to buy it, the bridegroom came, and those who were ready went with him into the wedding banquet, and the door was shut. Later the other bridesmaids came also, saying, 'Lord, lord, open to us.' But he replied, 'Truly I tell you, I do not know you.' Keep awake, therefore, for you know neither the day nor the hour.

Matthew 25:1-13

We must continue to prepare for Christ or we will be the foolish who are shut out. You see, it is one thing to know God and have Him fill your mind with wisdom and understanding, but we have yet to convert our hearts. If we want God to know us, we need to talk to God, and we need to open our hearts up to him. Truly, we must love God for Him to know us.

God created every one of us, and yes we are all His children, but He allows us to love Him back. We don't know when our final hour will be, and we don't know when we will see Jesus (the bridegroom). If our relationship with God isn't one of love, then truly He does not know you.

Are you ready to love God?

Love God

Everyone who loves is born of God and knows God. Whoever does not love does not know God, for God is love.

1 John 4:7-8

Growing up, I loved watching National Geographic programs, and the Discovery Channel. Living in Southwest Minnesota, although it's beautiful, the surrounding area is nothing like what you would see on these programs. I could transport myself from the flat prairie to the highest mountains, the thickest jungles, or the driest deserts. I would trade in squirrels, pheasants, and deer for elephants, lions, and crocodiles. The ability to see every corner of the planet and all the life that inhabits it helped me understand how big our planet was. Also, how great its creator is.

If we took a tour around our planet, we would see numerous geographical giants. Mount Everest reaches 29,032'[12] into the sky, the Nile River cuts 4,132 miles into the

---

[12] US Department of Commerce, National Oceanic and Atmospheric Administration. "The Highest Point above Earth's Center Is the Peak of Ecuador's Mount Chimborazo, Located Just One Degree South of the Equator Where Earth's Bulge Is Greatest." NOAA's National Ocean Service,

African continent,[13] the Sahara desert is so large that you could nearly fit the entirety of the continental U.S. within it,[14] and the deepest darkest point of the vast ocean is over 36,000' below.[15] Feel small yet? It would take a lifetime to travel around the world to experience all the beauties of our world. Although we can't all travel to every corner of the planet, that doesn't mean that we all can't participate in the greatest journey on Earth.

Mother Teresa famously stated that "the longest journey in the world is from our heart to our head".[16] When we look at how we build relationships, this becomes clear. For many, the end goal of a relationship is to find love. Whether it's a friend, or someone you have a crush on, the goal of love is present. The word love gets thrown around a lot in our modern communications. "I love ice cream", or "I love baseball" are common things we would say about numerous items, but of course, is not the same love that I have for my wife. When talking about love the Greeks broke it down into 4 types;

---

[13] "Nile River." Education.education.nationalgeographic.org

[14] "New Study Finds World's Largest Desert, the Sahara, Has Grown by 10 Percent since 1920." NSF. www.nsf.gov

[15] US Department of Commerce, National Oceanic and Atmospheric Administration. "How Deep Is the Ocean?" NOAA's National Ocean Service,

[16] Teresa, and Matthew Kelly. *Do something beautiful for God: The essential teachings of mother teresa: 365 daily reflections.* North Palm Beach, FL: Blue Sparrow, 2019.

Philia   -   Love between friendship
Storgi   -   Love between a family
Eros   -   Love between a couple
Agape   -   Love of God[17]

    Regardless, if I am trying to build a friendly relationship or a romantic one, the first step is always to build a better understanding of each other. It would be ridiculous to be in love with a stranger that you don't know or pick someone out of a crowd and say this is my new best friend. Whether it takes a day, a week, or a year, as long as we continue building our knowledge and understanding of one another, we will keep progressing toward love.

    Even though we throw around the term casually with everyday activities and items, it becomes harder to say it to another individual. It's even harder to actually mean it. In our modern culture, we have seen an increase in relationships built on physical desires instead of love. Movies, TV, and music have made it normal to sleep around and push off commitment. We even have game shows that have individuals get engaged to be married without ever seeing each other. Our culture makes a mockery out of love and marriage and the results of that are failed marriages, and increased single-parent households. The reason for this problem is that we are skipping the most important part of building a relationship and that is love. Without love, there is no commitment.

---

[17] "The Four Types of Love: Some Are Healthy, Some Are Not." University of Utah Health | University of Utah Health, May 12, 2023.

Why is it so hard to say I love you? We grow up believing that there are rules and expectations on how a relationship is supposed to be built. Many fear that if they say "I love you" too soon, they are rushing into it and might end the relationship. Can you fall in love too fast?

When my wife and I got engaged, we had only been dating 3 months and only knew each other for 5. I'm sure some people thought it was ridiculous and too fast, but can there really be a required amount of days to know you love someone? I always joke that I had to keep the family tradition alive. My parents were engaged after two months, and are continuing their happy marriage of 36 years. My grandma and grandpa were engaged after 3 months and were married for over 50 years before my grandfather passed. Love and marriage don't have a set timeline or formula because it changes from couple to couple. C. S. Lewis explains it perfectly when he says that "Love is friendship set on fire.'.[18] When we complete that incredible journey from our heads to our hearts, love flourishes.

At this point in our faith journey, we have been increasing our friendship with God while getting to know him, but we haven't begun to love Him yet. Hopefully, we are reading His word every day, getting to know our local faith community, and choosing to grow in understanding every day. For our friendship to catch on fire, we need to be fully committed to our relationship with God. Committing to someone that you can't see, feel, or hear can be a challenging obstacle. If we want to be able to receive God's love, we first

---

[18] Lewis, C.S. The theme of friendship in C. S. Lewis the four loves.

must complete the incredible journey from our head to our heart.

One thing we never have to doubt is the love that God has for us. As we go through the entire Bible we are reminded of this love when we see God's commitment to us. Through His covenant, we see that even in our faults, His love never trembles. We disobey His commands, break His covenant, and strive to be more like others than the people He made us to be, and yet, God still puts us first. Even with all our sins, and all our failures, He offered up His only son to die for us.

Christ's goal for us is that we all follow His example and reciprocate His love for one another.

> *Then Jesus told his disciples, 'If any want to become my followers, let them deny themselves and take up their cross and follow me.*
>
> *Matthew 16:24*

> *This is my commandment, that you love one another as I have loved you. No one has greater love than this, to lay one's life for one's friends.*
>
> *John 15:12-13*

Christ gave His life for us and for our sins. No matter our faults, failures, and weaknesses, Christ loves us. We must learn to follow His example and love someone who we sometimes feel is unworthy of that love because of their faults. That person is ourselves. For us to receive love, we first must be able to love ourselves. A commitment to loving ourselves must also come with a commitment to loving God. If we can not open up our hearts, then we are shutting God out as well. Jesus says,

> *'you shall love the Lord your God with all your heart, and with all your soul, and with all your mind, and with all your strength ... you shall love your neighbor as yourself. There is no other commandment greater than these.'*
>
> Mark 12:30-31

Our strength in loving God will open our hearts to love ourselves, and to love those around us. If we harden our hearts against God then we truly can not receive love.

To love oneself is not to live a life of vanity, or pride, but to see the beauty in God's creation in us all. When we look in the mirror, we should see the image and likeness of God with endless potential for good. Yet, sadly our cracks and blemishes creep in. We let this hinder us in our journey, and there are times we feel worthless. We stumble off the path and live a life on the lonely road of isolation and fill our minds with doubt and lies, thinking so little of ourselves. How could God ever love me after the things I have done, and all of my mistakes? I am broken and will permanently be scarred.

God never sees us as broken but as His children. He wants every one of us to run home to him. With His loving heart, He takes us in and puts us back together piece by piece. The cracks and blemishes are still there, but they are sealed by His love. God's parental love is explained in the beautiful parable of the prodigal son.

Then Jesus said, "There was a man who had two sons. The younger of them said to his father, 'Father, give me the share of the property that will belong to me.' So he divided his property between them. A few days later the younger son gathered all he had and traveled to a distant country, and there he squandered his property in dissolute living. When he had spent everything, a severe famine took place throughout that country, and he began to be in need. So he went and hired himself out to one of the citizens of that country, who sent him to his fields to feed the pigs. He would gladly have filled himself with the pods that the pigs were eating; and no one gave him anything. But when he came to himself he said, 'How many of my father's hired hands have bread enough and to spare, but here I am dying of hunger! I will get up and go to my father, and I will say to him, "Father, I have sinned against Heaven and before you; I am no longer worthy to be called your son; treat me like one of your hired hands."' So he set off and went to his father. But while he was still far off, his father saw him and was filled with compassion; he ran and put his arms around him and kissed him. Then the son said to him, 'Father, I have sinned against Heaven and before you; I am no longer worthy to be called your son.' But the father said to his slaves, 'Quickly, bring out a robe—the best one—and put it on him; put a ring on his finger and sandals on his feet. And get the fatted calf and kill it, and let us eat and celebrate; for this son of mine was dead and is alive again; he was lost and is found!' And they began to celebrate.

Luke 15:11-24

Oh, how comforting it is knowing we have a God who loves us more than any other creation. To know that through our faults, and failures, all He wants is for us to come home to Him and He can hold us in His arms. When we return from our path of isolation, only the greatest feast and celebration in God's Heavenly kingdom awaits.

How to Pray

Modern communication is constantly evolving. Probably the most noticeable part about it is that it's hardly in person. Between social media apps, messengers, and texting, we use our phones for the majority of our communication. Actual phone calls or face-timing have become almost inconvenient when you can gather information quicker simply by sending a text message. Half the time we don't even need to use words and can substitute our entire message with a thumbs-up emoji, or a laughing face. Some say history repeats itself so we must be going back to the stone age with cave drawings and grunts.

The biggest downside to modern communication is that it does become more impersonal. Sometimes the only words we speak to anyone in person may be our immediate family members and a select few coworkers or strangers. With all of our focus being on our phones, we don't always see the desire to interact with new individuals unless they are on social media. I always tease my wife because she is the opposite of this. It doesn't matter where we are, or what we are doing, but she will make conversation with anybody. As an introvert, this always surprises me. We will be waiting in line and she will casually spark up a conversation with the person standing next to her and have a lovely conversation. It's just part of her personality that I love so much. It's something I strive to become better at because you never know how a simple interaction with someone can change their day, and who knows, you might be able to brighten up their day and make them smile.

Now, I'm not saying that all modern communication is a bad thing. The ease of communicating over great distances, or the ability to have a large group in one conversation, makes maintaining relationships so much easier. In a time where family and friends can be scattered across many different states, or even around the world, it is incredible that we can talk almost instantaneously. It allows us to maintain these relationships, even if years go by without seeing someone. For example, one summer I worked with this incredible gentleman from Kenya. When he returned home, we were still able to email each other back and forth to stay in touch. Even 30 years ago, that would never have happened.

I always reflect on when my grandfather was in the army. The only communication that he had with his friends and family, for two years, was letters that he would send back and forth every few weeks and sometimes months. A simple double-sided letter to try and catch up on everything is nearly impossible. I'm sure he felt distanced and that he was missing out on so much not being home. The farther back you go, the more communication slows down. This did not mean that relationships were less important, but it made you cherish the time you had together and focus solely on the people you were with.

One tradition I wish would come back is the importance of gathering on Sunday. When my parents and grandparents were growing up, Sunday was the best day when families would gather together after church. Everyone was dressed up in their Sunday best and would spend the day talking, playing cards, and catching up, while the kids would run and play out in the yard. Sunday was a day that was a priority to focus on family and relationships.

Sadly, Sunday has become a day of self-desires and wants. A day only for TV, sweatpants, and junk food. God is usually low on the list of priorities in a modern home, especially when it's football season. Now, I love football more than any other sport. I never miss a Vikings game, and we are season ticket holders for the South Dakota State football team. There are a lot of weekends where we are driving all over the place from Friday to Sunday just to watch football, but where we draw the line is Sunday morning is devoted to

God. God comes first every single day, and especially on Sunday, we need to make the Mass a priority. When we lose the value of Sunday, it creeps into every other day. Too busy on a Sunday? How about a Tuesday? Soon, every day is too busy, and God is left alone.

Do you rest to work, or work to rest? What is our priority in life? The answer to this question is usually the driving force behind how we spend our weekends and spare time. If our careers are the driving force then we will use our spare time to rest so we can give more energy and focus to our jobs. Now, if our family and friends are the main priority then we will spend our days focusing on how to spend more time having fun with those around us. Work will always be there and there is always another project to get started, but we understand that it can wait until Monday. The weekend can just be focused on the weekend.

If we want to be successful at completing the incredible journey from our heads to our hearts, we need to make sure we have our goal in focus. If building a relationship with God is our priority, then He needs to be the priority in our lives. We need to make sure that every day we are making the effort to reach out to him.

Prayer life is difficult to start and maintain. Just like any relationship, communication is a fundamental building block. Could you go a full day without speaking to your spouse? How about not saying "Good morning", "I love you", or "Good night?" We have to remember how much God loves us, and how His love is unwavering. Yet, how often do we spend days and even months without speaking to him? All He wants is to hear us say "I love you". Yet, we devote our attention to material things that can never love us back, and will never fill us with as much joy as God can.

    I will be honest, I was never good at praying. I loved filling my mind with knowledge of the faith, and how to defend it. I loved listening to scholars break down the bible, and all the beautiful connections and references throughout. My mind was fully Catholic and fully devoted to God. I knew that this was real and that this was important, but my heart was never converted. Even when I got married, I still struggled.

    My prayer life changed by the grace of God when I received a random text message from my uncle. The local church had established perpetual adoration at one of their school chapels. There were a few openings they were still trying to fill, so he reached out to me to see if I would be interested. Now, of course, the open times wouldn't be considered high-demand time, and I ended up locking in the 3 AM time slot every Friday morning. I would go to the chapel and pray before the Eucharist.

    Now, I had done adoration before in school or on church trips but this was the first time in my life that I was truly alone with the Eucharist. No large crowd, or music playing in the background. It was in that silence that God finally reached my heart. I could finally feel that bridge between my head and my heart finally being established. I just started to talk to him. I unloaded all of my grief, fears, and worries. I cried out everything that I was thankful for, and how unworthy I felt that He had blessed me with such a great life, even with all my failures. From that time on, it became so much easier to talk with Him and continue breaking down the wall that I had put up around my heart. I always joke that this experience was like when you have two kids that can't get along, so you sit them down in timeout and they can't leave until they talk things out. God and I needed a timeout session.

A lot of times, we treat our prayer life like it's a first date. What am I going to say? I don't want to say the wrong thing or insult the other person. I mean what if we run out of things to talk about? Trust me, as a shy kid, who hardly spoke until junior high, these fears ran through my head anytime I attempted to talk to girls, and it usually didn't work out so well. We always put so much pressure on that first interaction and fear that it's an all-or-nothing approach.

Luckily Jesus shows us how we should approach our prayer life with the Father.

> *Your Father knows what you need before you ask him. Pray then in this way:*
>
> *Our Father in Heaven, hallowed be your name. Your Kingdom come. Your will be done, on Earth as it is in Heaven. Give us this day our daily bread. And forgive us our debts, as we forgive our debtors. And do not bring us to the time of trial, but rescue us from the evil one.*
>
> *Matthew 6:8-13*

How beautiful and perfect this prayer is. Yes, we should continue praying the "Our Father" daily as we do at Mass, or throughout the Rosary, but what about our personal prayers?

The beauty of the "Our Father" is how it is structured. You see, it's not just a bunch of words that sound good, and it's not simply a wish list. The bones of this prayer are how we should structure all of our prayers to God.

When we begin our prayers, it should never just be "Father, please let the Vikings win the Super Bowl." That obviously doesn't work. It should be a sign of our gratitude and love towards him. Recognition of all the great things He has done for us, and that we are at the mercy of Him so that His will be done. When I pray it will look something like this. "Father, thank you for all the many blessings in my life. You are my strength, my light, and my redeemer. I am your servant so that your light can shine in the world." Completely different, but the bones are still there.

This is where the "wish list" begins. I do love that Jesus states that God already knows what we are bringing to the table, but He still wants us to ask (We will discuss this in more detail soon when we look at forgiveness and Reconciliation). What should we ask of the Lord? The age-old question, does God care about football? Probably not, because He is most likely receiving the same prayer from the other team. Does God want me to be rich and famous? Once again, God's track record with wealth doesn't make it too realistic that He desires His people to be billionaires. You see God isn't some genie that we get to make wishes with. If that were the case, then we are using God, not loving him.

When Jesus says "Give us our daily bread," we must look deeper. Now, if you are suffering from poverty then you might just need help feeding your family. For those of us that are just cruising through life trying to make sense of what

God wants from us, "Our daily bread," comes from our weaknesses. We need to self-reflect where we have stumbled and failed. Maybe we are battling porn addiction, maybe we find ourselves quick to anger or are too dependent on alcohol. What do you find yourself crying out to the Lord saying? "Lord give me strength for I am weak in the moments of isolation. Give me patience and calm my heart when it leads to anger. Help me love as you love, and help me share that love with your people."

Our hearts are now opened up to the Lord, and we have laid it all out there. He knows our faults and weaknesses, but He doesn't treat us like failures but as His sons and daughters. The best way to think about it, is He just wants to give us a big 'ol hug.

After confessing our sins and desires, we should ask for God's forgiveness just like in the "Our Father". More importantly, we must forgive those who hurt us. Not an easy thing to do and it might take some time as you heal, but it is something we all must do. "Lord, forgive me for turning from you when I feel alone. I know that I am never alone and you are always by my side. Lord, I pray for those who have hurt me and have made me feel weak. Listen to their prayers and be by their side so that we will both be with you in Heaven. "

As we end our prayers, ask for God's protection from sin and temptation. "Lord, protect me as you walk with me through this day and every day. Defend me in battle and be a lamp upon my feet."

Together when I kneel before Mass, my prayers look like this;

"Father, thank you for all the many blessings in my life. You are my strength, my light, and my redeemer. I am your servant so that your light can shine in the world. Lord, give me strength for I am weak in the moments of isolation. Give me patience and calm my heart when it leads to anger. Help me love as you love, and help me share that love with your people. Lord, forgive me for turning from you when I feel alone. I know that I am never alone and you are always by my side. Lord, I pray for those who have hurt me and have made me feel weak. Listen to their prayers and be by their side so that we will both be with you in Heaven. Lord, protect me as you walk with me through this day and every day. Defend me in battle and be a lamp upon my feet."

It's just that simple. Recognition, confession, forgiveness, and protection. These are the key elements to improve our prayer life. We need to focus on how to heal our hearts, and how to help others. Our prayers should never be about money, fame, or glory.

When we look at the Mass, it is structured in the same way. When we are in front of the Blessed Sacrament, the first thing we do is genuflect or kneel before the Lord. This is a sign of respect and honor to our God who has given us everything. When I kneel, I always say a simple prayer, "My Lord and my God. Defend me in battle and be a lamp upon my feet." Then, I kneel before the Lord and recite my prayer, then healing can begin.

Forgiveness

One of the biggest distinctions between Catholics and other Christian faiths is the Sacrament of Reconciliation. The biggest criticism that Catholics get is, "Why confess your sins to a priest when I can confess them directly to God?" This is true and something that Catholics wouldn't argue with. For example, if a soldier is overseas, and nowhere near a priest if he confesses his sins during his prayers, we have faith that God is listening and will forgive him. Especially if that soldier finds his life to be at risk, we want his soul to be filled with grace.

So why the priest then? Well although we aren't all soldiers, we are all fighting a war. A spiritual war for our soul between God and Satan. The priest is our greatest human ally in this fight. From the outside, it could look like we believe that the priest is forgiving our sins, but that's not what we believe. It is God forgiving us through the priest. Just like God worked through His Apostles, He works through the priests today.

That still doesn't answer my question about confessing directly to God. My response to that would be that most of our sin is committed in darkness or isolation and although God may forgive us when we ask for forgiveness in the darkness, that doesn't necessarily fix us. At least not permanently. A lot of the time we want to hide our sin and keep it in the darkness.

My sister loves sharing this story about when she convinced my brother to move outside into the playset because he broke one of Mom's dishes when they were kids. He was convinced that she would be mad and that this would never be forgiven. He gathered all of his things and hid in the playset for fear of Mom. Of course, Mom gets home, sees that he is sitting outside, and is just confused why something that could be fixed caused so much fear. She sat down and talked with him and he moved back into the house before it was dark.

Seems silly but our relationship with God is the same. When we break the rules or feel that we have made God angry we tend to run away or hide from Him. We naturally feel safer because if we stay in the darkness, we won't be reprimanded. Who is telling us this lie? Well, Satan himself is telling us that "God is an angry and vengeful God and could never love a sinner like you". Has this thought ever run through your head? (Just to be clear, I am not calling my sister the devil, it's only an analogy. I love my sister and she is a beautiful, strong, and wonderful mother, sister, daughter, and wife. Hopefully, that covers my back).

Sin tends to become a routine. Although, we feel so much grief and disgust in ourselves every time we find ourselves committing the same sin and cry out to God that we are sorry, we still feel broken. Wanting to rid ourselves of this sin, we find comfort in the darkness and fear exposing it to the light. Eventually, we stop crying out to Him and just hide in our sins. When we do this, we are allowing the Devil to win the war for our souls. The challenge of confessing to a priest is you have a personal relationship with that priest and you are so scared to disappoint them, that you keep it hidden. Just like my brother wanted to hide from my Mother.

It takes strength and courage to fall to your knees and repent (change our thinking). Then, face God and tell Him your sins. That's the courage that it takes to walk into the confessional. Now, traditionally there is a screen between you and the priest but in our church, you have the option to go face-to-face. I have always confessed face-to-face, one because I'm from a small town, so not like he won't know who I am by the sound of my voice anyway, but because it is more impactful to look at them face-to-face and see God. It is such a vulnerable position, although more challenging, it feels more genuine. I am not hiding from the sins that I have committed, but truly owning my mistakes. Usually, my head is facing the floor as I list off my sins, but then something changes. The priest begins to speak about how we can combat these challenges. As you look at him and listen to his guidance, you finally start to realize that there is an 'off-ramp' to this wicked lifestyle you've been living. His words are uplifting, supportive, and constructive. Then through the grace of God, your sins are forgiven. You are sent forth filled with this grace to change your life for the better.

The challenge is always how long we stay in that state of grace. What even is grace? Some of you might think it's the prayer before a meal. Although essential, that's not what we are talking about. The grace I am talking about is the grace that the Angel Gabriel addresses when he visits Mary saying *"Hail, full of Grace; the Lord is with you"(Luke 1:28)*. To keep it simple, grace is a state of perfect communion with God. As Catholics, we enter this state of grace at our Baptism, through

Reconciliation, when we receive the Eucharist and all the sacraments. Each sacrament helps us break down that wall of sin and brings us back into perfect communion with God. The problem is that this isn't sustainable with our human hearts. We could leave the confessional filled with God, but then trip on our way out of the church and begin to swear or take the Lord's name in vain. Poof, it's gone. Now that doesn't mean you quickly run back up to the priest and start over, but yet it's the lifelong marathon of desiring to be in communion with God. So as we live our lives, we need to ask ourselves, are we seeking that union with God, or do we allow our sin to create a bigger wedge between us and God?

Nothing is more rewarding than to feel like you have overcome a great sin. Maybe you're an alcoholic and you just hit a year of sobriety. Maybe you cuss and swear like a sailor and now you're down to just the occasional slip-up of the tongue. The biggest mistake we can make is thinking that "I" have overcome my sin. We need to give credit where it is due. Yes, when we overcome sin it is by the choice of our free will, but the strength to overcome the temptation to sin comes directly from God. We must give Him thanks and praise for giving us the strength to overcome and conquer. If we don't, we just replace the previous sin with that of vanity and pridefulness.

Whether you are preparing for Reconciliation, or are opening up your heart through your prayers at home, there are certain aspects that we need to understand to fully make a true confession. We have already talked about asking for forgiveness, but for us to be forgiven we also need to be willing to forgive. That is the instruction that immediately follows the teaching of the "Our Father".

> *For if you forgive others their trespasses, your Heavenly Father will also forgive you; but if you do not forgive others, neither will your Father forgive your trespasses.*
>
> Matthew 6:14-15

How can I receive something that I am not willing to also give? That would make me a hypocrite. Yet, how often do we catch ourselves saying both, "Lord, please forgive me for I am weak and have made a mistake," but then to someone else say, "What that person did is unforgivable, and they deserve the harshest punishment." It is an easy trap to fall into. The stubbornness of heart and anger can fully control us. I'm not saying that forgiveness is easy because there are horrible things that people can do to us and to those we love. Many people are victims of sexual abuse, have lost family members to drunk driving, or even had their entire lives stolen from them through fraud. There are truly great evils in this world, but we must bring love into this world instead of more hate.

    I always talk about how the saints are the perfect role models for us as sinners to get closer to God. All the saints had some form of sin or struggle they had to overcome on their way to sainthood. When we look at the challenge of forgiving others who have harmed us, there is no more relevant saint than the newly canonized St. John Paul II.

On May 13, 1981, St. John Paul II was driving through St. Peter's Square in Vatican City. With a large crowd surrounding the Pope's Jeep, everybody went into a panic when gunshots were fired. The Pope had been shot in the chest and was in critical condition. The man who shot him was Mehmet Ali Agca, a Turkish assassin. Agca was detained by Vatican security and sentenced to life in prison where he would be held in Rome.[19]

It took over 3 months for St. John Paul II to recover from his wounds and be able to leave the hospital. During this time, St. John Paul II didn't allow hate to fill his heart, nor did he try to forget his assassin. Instead, he did the saintly act of praying for him. He even encouraged all to "pray for my brother ... whom I have sincerely forgiven."[20] In 1983, St. John Paul II formally met him in prison and the two started a friendship. St. John Paul II carried his love for Agca for decades, even making a push for him to be pardoned.[21]

It's remarkable to see a modern saint live as Christ asks us all to live. It immediately brings to mind the actions of Christ as He was being crucified. As an innocent man, Jesus hung on a cross dying the most gruesome and torturous death designed in human history. He had been scourged, stripped, beaten, spit on, mocked, and was about to die. Yet, He looked up to the Heavens and cried out, *"Father, forgive*

---

[19] Vogele, Markus. "An Eyewitness Recalls the Attempt on St John Paul II's Life." Catholic News Agency,

[20] Saltandlighttv. "JP II, We Love You - Pope John Paul II Forgives His Would-Be Assassin." Salt + Light Media.

[21] Ibid

them; for they do not know what they are doing."(Luke 23:24) Even when facing death, the mercy of God is unwavering.

There is still one more challenge we need to overcome if we want to make a great Reconciliation and truly transform our lives. We know that we need to repent and ask for forgiveness, we need to forgive those who have caused us harm, but the most difficult challenge we face is forgiving ourselves.

Why is it so hard to forgive ourselves? Well to put it simply, we know every bad thing we have ever done. Our hearts weigh heavy carrying the guilt of our sins, and the understanding of how many times we stop and think "I know God doesn't want me to do this act", and we do it anyway. We look at ourselves and just think, "How could God ever love a sinner like me?" "You don't deserve to be forgiven." This is usually the obstacle that keeps us out of the confessional in the first place.

Every sin we commit is like a brick being used to build a wall around our hearts. As we let that wall build, we keep asking ourselves, "How could God ever love me?" We hide behind our wall. We are sitting by ourselves as if in a jail cell. Yet, on the other side of that wall, Jesus is listening to us cry out and you can hear Him saying, "I love you, but you need to love yourself. Allow me to love you." You are faced with a choice as you sit in your cell. I can sit in isolation or I can tear down this wall.

Within your cell, you see a mirror hanging on the wall. As you stare at your reflection, you think of your faults, blemishes, and weaknesses. You begin to think, *"I am weak, but the Lord is strong and He is with me. I can do all things through him who strengthens me (Philippians 4:13)"*

You turn to the voice of the Lord desperate to be with him. Brick by brick you start to tear down the wall. It is a challenge and you are tempted to quit but you're focused on His voice and will not be deterred. With each brick, you see more and more of Christ. As you remove the last brick, you drop to your knees in front of him. Sitting next to you lies the mound of your sins. He embraces you and says, "You are loved, and you are forgiven."

As He hugs you, the mound of sins is removed. Your heart is filled with love and is free from the restraints of sin. Beneath your feet, the bricks have been laid to form a path behind you. Showing where you have been, and your journey up to this point.

Your sin is a part of your journey. There is no way to remove them from your mind and forget they ever happened, but instead of letting our sins separate us from God, let us always see them as a part of our story of how we returned to God. None of us are perfect, and our paths are crooked and bumpy. If we look to the Lord that path will always be behind us, and the light of Christ will guide us moving forward.

> *"I am the light of the world. Whoever follows me will never walk in darkness but will have the light of Life."*
>
> *John 8:12*

Forms of Prayer

When my wife and I were engaged a certain question kept being asked, "What is your love language?" "Huh?" Friends and family would ask us if we had taken the quiz, or had to do any reading on love languages. It was brought up again when we were talking to other engaged couples in our pre-marriage classes. Every time my wife and I just sort of shrugged our shoulders and thought it was silly.

We finally broke down and looked into what everyone was fussing about. Turns out, this love language quiz shows you how you communicate love with those around you and is like a personality test for your love life. It breaks down love languages into five different categories on how the individual best interprets and shows love. So when people kept asking us if we had taken the quiz yet, what they were really asking was, "How compatible are you guys?" So what are the five love languages anyway? They are; words of affirmation, physical touch, receiving of gifts, quality time, and acts of service.[22]

If words of affirmation are your love language then you probably enjoy giving spontaneous messages, or cards, and use language to show your appreciation. *"O Romeo,*

---

[22] Member, UAGC Staff. "The Psychology behind the 5 Love Languages." UAGC.

Romeo, wherefore art thou Romeo?"[23] That sort of thing. You are someone who encourages those around you and shows attention when listening to others. If someone doesn't show appreciation for your efforts or gives you criticism, that could be something that upsets you.

Physical touch is pretty on the nose. Words aren't important but physical touch shows your love. Hugs, kisses, holding hands, or cuddling. Anything that people might roll their eyes at if you do it too much in public. If someone gives you a cold shoulder or doesn't want to sit right next to you, that may be something you take harshly.

Receiving gifts is usually viewed as being one of the most thoughtful and yet maybe polarizing love languages. Some people are great at thinking of gifts and love giving them to others, and then there are people like me who are terrible at it. If you ever ask me what I want for Christmas or my birthday, it's the same thing every year, "I don't need anything." It's not because I'm a minimalist or trying to humble myself and say, "Your presence is enough of a present." If I'm honest it's because I genuinely don't know and if I think of something I do want, I buy it. I come from a family that has grown out of gift-giving once grandkids entered the family, but marrying into my wife's family, they were all about gifts. On birthdays, holidays, or Mother's Day, it seemed like we were constantly planning the next gift. It was foreign to me, but that was how they showed their appreciation towards each other. For those whose love language is receiving gifts even the small gestures are huge.

---

[23] Shakespeare, William. 1993. Romeo and Juliet. Dover Thrift Editions. Mineola, NY: Dover Publications.

Maybe they will randomly Venmo their best friend that just says "Starbucks" on it with a smiley face emoji. Now if you forget special occasions, or are unenthusiastic when you are receiving a gift from them, you're going to make them upset.

Quality time is probably what most people assume their grandma and grandpa's language is. A long uninterrupted conversation which is mostly one-on-one. It's a priority of spending time together whether that is watching movies, going for walks, or any other personal activity. I remember hearing commentary on an elderly couple sitting together eating breakfast not saying a word. The initial comment was, "Well they finally ran out of things to say to each other", but the reality of that moment is so much more beautiful. Even without saying a word, their presence shows how much they love each other because the absence of the other leaves them feeling alone or empty.

The final love language is acts of service. Going above and beyond to help lighten the load for someone or show them that you want to help. Doing chores around the house without being asked, or making a special meal for them. Our love is shown through our actions. If we always put ourselves first, this love language is hard to connect with.

So which language do you respond to the best? Which one do you find the easiest to show? As we went through this list, I'm sure a few different languages jumped out at you. Maybe a few of them were relatable. For most of us, we are a combination of different love languages. When my wife and I were first married, our language was quality time and physical touch. Now as our relationship has developed and our family started to grow, I would say acts of service have started to take over as the number 2 language in our relationship. It's common for our love languages to evolve and change over time.

So how does this relate to God? Well, the whole focus of this book is to develop our relationship with God, and just like our relationship with our spouses, family, or friends, there are different languages to communicate our love for God.

We talked about the "Our Father" is how God showed us how to pray, but that doesn't mean that is the only prayer. Just like how there is more than one love language, there are numerous ways to pray and show our love for God.

One of the most common prayers that Catholics will pray daily is the Rosary. Now, the Rosary isn't a singular prayer, but a series of prayers. The Rosary starts with the "Apostles' Creed" and then is composed of a sequence of "Our Fathers," "Hail Marys," "Glory Be," and the "Fatima Prayer." As a whole, the Rosary is a devotion in honor of our Blessed Mother Mary. The Rosary came into existence gradually over centuries, but it is believed to have been a common Catholic practice for over 800 years.

The challenge of the Rosary is to not turn it into mindless repetition but to truly use it as a tool to focus on our prayer, and on the Word of God. When we begin to pray, we should have a person, cause, or devotion in mind. We can have something for the Rosary as a whole, or devote each decade to praying for something different. For example, you could pray for your family, for an increase in vocations, for teachers and students, for unborn children, and for the souls in purgatory. Each has a decade to focus on and pray for.

Another form of prayer that goes well with the Rosary is reading scripture. Whether we are reading the "Bible in a Year", reading the daily Mass readings, or praying the Psalms every day, it's important to take time to stop and reflect on what we are reading. What is God trying to teach me? What can I learn from this to help me in my day-to-day life? Use the bible as a phone line to God.

One of my favorite daily prayers is a Scriptural Rosary which combines these two forms of prayer. This is done by expanding upon the mysteries of the Rosary and adding scripture before each "Hail Mary." Wait, what are the mysteries of the Rosary? Every day of the week has a set mystery out of four that are used, unlike the crime mystery you might be thinking of, the mysteries of the Rosary are far from unknown. The beauty of the mysteries is that they are events of the life of Christ and we are called to reflect on them. The mysteries are joyful, luminous, sorrowful, and glorious. These four mysteries stretch from the annunciation to the coronation.

The beauty of the Scriptural Rosary is instead of breaking down the mysteries into five key events, we instead get the mysteries from 50 different lines of scripture. It helps slow down our pacing and expands upon our reflection of the life of Christ.

Whether you are praying the traditional Rosary, or reading scripture, the key element is reflection and meditation. Once again, we don't want the prayer to be a chore, and we don't want it to turn into a race to the finish line so we can check it off our list of things to do. Instead, we have to make sure that we are coming into our prayer with the intention of healing, growing, or strengthening a loving relationship. When we recite the memorized prayers, are we focusing on what we are saying? When we read scripture, are we playing bible roulette or do we have a set guide we are following each day? Especially when reading scripture, it can get messy, or confusing. It is important to take pause breaks to allow your heart and mind to sync up. What do you think God is teaching us at this moment, and what is striking your heart the most?

    A great way to look at your "structured prayer" is as an icebreaker. A way to get the conversation moving. If we want a relationship with God, we should be able to have a better conversation with him. God doesn't demand that we follow a set formula when speaking to him.

    If you're looking for something different to mix up your prayer life, I would encourage listening and participating in meditations. I'm not talking about listening to a calm stream and start humming until you have an out-of-body experience, but a meditation where you walk with Christ. Are you preparing for lent and want to get off on the right foot? Then, think about what it would be like to walk with Jesus in the wilderness for 40 days. Think of the heat, imagine the hunger, and imagine the pain. Imagine what Christ looks like while he's fasting. Is He angry, happy, or is He at peace? At any moment throughout scripture, we should take time to pause and place ourselves in the lesson. Not at the center, but as a witness. You will be amazed at the connection you have with God when you meditate on being a witness to scripture.

For thousands of years, music has been a traditional form of prayer. We see it in the Psalms, and still throughout the Mass today. Chants, songs, and choirs enhance the prayer experience. Now, there is a difference between listening to the most recent Christian music versus a Psalm, or a church hymn. The difference is one is a prayer and one is a worship song. Both are very great elements but don't satisfy the same goal. If you listen to Christian radio on your drive to and from work, that doesn't substitute your prayers for the day. This does open up an avenue for God to speak to you. Now if you are listening to daily Mass, reading, and singing along with the Psalm, or if you add music to begin or end your prayer time to calm your mind, that is a wonderful use of the gifts and talents presented in Christian music.

At the pinnacle of prayer life is the most powerful and important way of praying, and that is the adoration of the Eucharist. Adoration is when the Eucharist is on display in a monstrance (sun-looking contraption). Whether it's in a church or a chapel, being in the presence of Christ's Body is the best place to pray. It was in an adoration chapel that I truly built my relationship with God. It wasn't because I said a Rosary every day, or read a new book every week, but because I started having a conversation with God.

It is common when in adoration, we "fill" in our time with reading scripture, listening to Christian music, walking through meditation, or reciting prayers. These are all various forms of prayer, but it steals from what is important. If we are devoting an hour to God, we tend to try and make sure our minds are constantly going to make that hour go by a little quicker, but are we truly embracing the gift that is present before us?

When my wife and I first got exposed to a Steubenville conference, we were chaperones and boy was that an experience. The speakers were phenomenal, the band was wonderful, and the entire weekend was such a powerful experience to see thousands of Catholics gather together united by their love for God. Yet, at one of the Masses, I caught myself thinking, "I hope this isn't the best Mass of their lives." That seems a bit negative, doesn't it? Well, the reason I say that is because there is so much added to the Mass to make it an elevated experience. There is a live band, thousands of people singing, a fog machine on stage, and backlighting behind the altar. I just didn't want the "extra" to be what made the kids love the Mass.

When we think of the Mass, I always think of it as a gift. We can put the gift in a large box, wrap it in shiny, wrapping paper, put a massive bow on it, and when we open it there is a card that sings. As spectacular as that would be, it has no impact on what the actual gift is. The gift could be in a small box that fits in your pocket with a top and a bottom that, although might not match, miraculously fit together, and there's a "To:" and "From:" note scribbled in pencil. Same gift, just a different presentation.

When you remove the band, the fog, the lights, and the people, the greatest gift is revealed to be the Eucharist. That same Eucharist is present in a small town chapel as it is in St. Peter's Basilica. I pray that the many young kids who were having a life-changing experience that weekend came closer to the gift, not the presentation.

If our focus is on the wrong thing, will we have the same experience when it's our neighbor trying her best to hit the high notes, a priest that is hard to hear over the muffled speakers or the pianist that is guaranteed to miss a few notes? We must always remember that the greatest gift is present in the Tabernacle and in the silence of our hearts.

So whenever we are at adoration, when we are devoting 10 minutes to praying to God, we must welcome silence. Prayer is a conversation with God, and we must give Him His chance to speak. All the beautiful forms of prayer are crucial to building that relationship but it isn't until we sit in God's presence, surrounded by silence, that we can hear Him say, "I love you too."

Heaven on Earth

As stated previously, the pinnacle of our prayer life, and the holiest moment of our lives, is when in the presence of the Eucharist. This is why the celebration of the Mass is so crucial. Whether it is a short daily Mass, a holy day, or your weekly obligation, that time spent in the Mass is spectacular. It is nothing short of Heaven on Earth.

Sorry, I should have led with a "SPOILER ALERT" or "BREAKING NEWS" so that the shock of hearing this didn't knock the book right out of your hand. Obviously, I'm being sarcastic because you would assume that everyone would associate the Mass with Heaven, but let's look at the facts before making assumptions.

According to a "General Social Survey", performed by the U.S. Government, over the 50 years before the pandemic, Catholic Mass attendance had been cut in half, down to roughly 24% of Catholics that attend Mass every week.[24] At the same time, Catholics that never attend Mass, nearly doubled, reaching 22%. The decline in attendance has continued in our post-pandemic world. Many report an additional 25-30% decline in attendance after the 2020 pandemic. These numbers line up with the discovery that 69% of Catholics view the Eucharist as a mere symbol.[25] A direct contradiction to Catholic teaching.

So if Catholics aren't attending Mass and are losing their faith, then do they still believe in their salvation? What exactly does the average Christian believe Heaven is? According to a Pew Research Center study from November 2021, the majority of adults in the U.S. believe that in Heaven, you will meet God, have perfect health, be free from suffering, and be reunited with loved ones.[26] Other common views but not the majority, were being reunited with pets (100% agree), being able to watch life on Earth, ability to become an

---

[24] Joan Frawley Desmond "The Catholic Church Battles to Fill the Pews." NCR.

[25] Smith, Gregory A. "Just One-Third of U.S. Catholics Agree with Their Church That Eucharist Is Body, Blood of Christ." Pew Research Center, August 5, 2019. Pewresearch.org

[26] Mitchell, Travis. "2. Views on the Afterlife." Pew Research Center's Religion & Public Life Project, November 23, 2021. Pewresearch.org

angel, or even stop existence altogether.[27] If you ask someone what Heaven will be like, they might describe it as a grand city in the clouds, with angels flying around. Peter is standing by the pearly gates of Heaven, and we each will live in mansions on streets paved with gold. Many popular culture references to Heaven, may make us believe that when we get to Heaven we will have powers and can have anything we want and make things appear out of thin air. I would caution against striving for a Heaven that indulges in the 7 deadly sins like greed, pride, envy, or gluttony but one that enhances the 7 gifts of the Holy Spirit (wisdom, knowledge, counsel, fortitude, understanding, piety, and fear of the Lord).

So what do Catholics believe? The Catechism of the Catholic Church states;

> *Those who die in God's grace and friendship and are perfectly purified live forever with Christ. They are like God forever, for they "see him as he is," face to face.*
>
> CCC 1023

Can you imagine what that will be like? When we leave the comforts of this world and finally get to see God face-to-face. It gives me goosebumps just thinking about it, but yet it's nothing new to the human experience. It's one of the only things that every human on Earth goes through. Our births.

After our conception, we are bursting with life as we rapidly begin to grow each day. Our mother's womb is a nurturing home that supports our lives and provides

---

[27] Ibid

everything we need. Even as we grow and develop our senses, we are still lost in confusion as we sit in the darkness. We don't understand how we were created, but we know that someone outside of these walls must be our creator. How much love the creator must have for us to give us this life? Is there life outside of this place we ponder? As we sat alone in the womb, we began to hear this muffled voice, and it almost seemed like it was talking to us. We can't understand what she is saying but she sounds sweet. We are drawn into the woman's voice and although we don't know what she looks like, and we've never seen her, we love her. Her sweet voice makes us leap. We long to be with her, but we do not know the day nor the hour. Finally, our day has come.

From out of the darkness we see nothing but pure light. Then once again, we hear that sweet voice that we love so much, and for the first time, we look into our mother's eyes. Her beauty glows as she says, "I love you." Her voice has never been clearer, and her arms wrap around you. I came from a place of limitations, but now I know that this is why I was created. To rest in this woman's arms.

In this new world, we live in the light side by side with our mother. We grow in wisdom and understanding of how the world works. We develop senses that were impossible in the womb, and we are surrounded by our brothers, sisters, friends, and family, all of who love us because of our mother. For when they look at us they see the mother and I see the mother in them.

This is how the mystery of God works in our lives on Earth.

This perfect life with the Most Holy Trinity - this Communion of life and love with the Trinity, with the Virgin Mary, the angels, and all the blessed - is called "Heaven." Heaven is the ultimate end and fulfillment of the deepest human longing, the state of supreme, definitive happiness.

CCC 1024

So why is the Mass so important? Because it is Heaven on Earth. For one hour, we get a glimpse at Heaven as we hear the voice of God, and we receive His Body and Blood. Remember, that the grace of God is being in perfect union with him. That is why the Eucharist is so special and so crucial to our prayer lives and our relationship with God.

So how well do we cherish this opportunity to be with God? Are we thankful for the opportunity to be in His presence and communion with Him? Do we thank Him for freeing us from the shackles of our sin? Do we dress up for Mass to celebrate His victory in this Eucharist because He is the risen King? Sadly, too often we choose to celebrate Earthly desires instead. Sometimes we drink too much on Saturday and are too hungover to go to church, or we would hate for others to judge us because of the state we are in. Maybe we are heading up to watch an NFL game, or we are hosting a party to watch the game at our homes and just don't have a second to spare. Maybe we had a hard work week, and we spent Saturday volunteering at a waffle feed raising money for the local Special Olympics, and since we did so much good on Saturday, we just really needed a day to rest.

Every time we are faced with the choice of not attending Mass, we can be assured that the devil himself is behind the temptation to skip. Even when we are at the busiest time of our lives with kids, school, sports, jobs, and all the chaos that life throws at us, there is always an opportunity to pray and allow God to remove all the stress and weight off your shoulders. When we are at our lowest because we got dumped, fired from our job, didn't get into the school we wanted, or a loved one has been taken from us, we are allowed to unload our hearts to God and allow Him to wrap His arms around us. When we have fallen out of sobriety, when we've caught ourselves looking at pornography, or whenever we allow the darkness of sin to blind us, we must let the mercy of the Lord shine through the darkness.

> *I used to believe that prayer changed things, but now I know prayer changes us, and we change things.*
>
> *St. Mother Teresa*

Suffering and Doubt

"The City of Tracy is gone." These were the words that my grandfather uttered to his family as he returned home after observing the wreckage from one of the most devastating tornadoes in Minnesota's history.

On June 13th, 1968 a violent F5 tornado ripped through the heart of our little town of Tracy. With winds over 300 mph and a diameter of destruction 2 blocks wide, anything that lay in its path was destroyed. Over 100 homes were destroyed and over 100 more were damaged. Businesses were completely lost, and the elementary school was left in ruins. Heavy boxcars were tossed nearly 300 yards

Photo taken by Eric Lantz

away. The greatest damage was the 9 individuals who lost their lives to the storm.

When we are faced with tragedy, devastation, and life-altering news, how well do we handle it? What emotions do we find ourselves facing? Some of us may have had these hurdles or roadblocks rattle our lives, and some of us can only imagine. I have had a fairly sheltered life up to this point when it comes to Earth-shattering tragedy.

Let's revisit my little town of Tracy after the tragedy of the tornado. In our church's centennial book, they have numerous reports and photos of the aftermath. One photo captured my attention. (Below)

Where would you even begin? I can't imagine what it must have been like to crawl out of your basement and step into a whole new world. Cars flipped, trees uprooted, and homes completely destroyed. There's no way to salvage your home, all your belongings are gone, and you feel completely helpless. What sorrow and grief those people must have felt.

Why does God allow suffering to take place? I thought God was supposed to be all good and take care of His people. Does He even care? When tragedy strikes, we are faced with the emotions of fear, doubt, and anger. For some, this might even lead to a feeling of hate towards God. The tragedy is the toughest test we face, and it reveals what kind of foundation we have built our faith on.

The question of evil in the world is the groundwork for many to lose their faith and belief in God. Fr. Mike Schmitz tells a beautiful story of God's relationship with the world and the evil within it.[28] God is pure good, and can not create evil. For example, take the sun. A pure source of light and warmth, but when it's dark out or cold, does that mean that the sun does not exist? Is the sun the creator of darkness and cold temperatures? During the winter months, when the sun has less power and the climate turns into a frigid tundra, is it because the sun is punishing us? Of course not, we know that during the winter months, we are tilted away from the sun and don't receive the direct sunlight we do during the summer. Winter is a result of our relationship with the sun, and how we are positioned with it.

The presence of evil in the world isn't a creation of God, or even an absence of God in the world because He is a

---

[28] Stefanick, Chris, and Ron Bolster. *Chosen: Whats Your Story God? & Creation and the Fall Part 1*. Ascension , 2016.

vengeful God, but it is the direct result of us abandoning him. When we try to live in a world without God, it's like living in a world without the sun. It would be cold, dark, miserable, and uninhabitable. The big lie is that we can't do anything about evil, we're all in it together, or that there is no God so why waste your time with that religious stuff?

This is the dilemma of free will. God created us with free will so that we aren't just mindless robots or pets that He controls. If we were, then yes, we would live in a world of pure goodness, but it wouldn't be by choice. It wouldn't be something that we would enjoy or appreciate. You see the beauty of free will is that we get to CHOOSE God, but because of free will, we welcome evil into the world. The hard part about free will is that our choices can have both a positive and negative impact on the lives of those around us. For example, if a group of college kids is out having fun drinking, and the end of the night arrives, they realize they aren't fit to drive. They are faced with a choice. On one side, they can call a designated driver, an Uber, or walk home, if it's close enough. The other choice is to drive themselves which could lead to them getting a ticket, an accident, or even ending someone's life. If someone loses their life to a drunk driver, is that because God was absent, or was it a result of the choices that were madqe? Far too often we abuse our free will. Take a moment and look back at human history at different scandals, wars, or persecutions. Then, ask yourself where free will was abused.

Now, what about natural disasters? Free will didn't cause that tornado to form. That is clear evidence that God allows suffering and doesn't do anything about it, isn't it? If a child gets cancer, that clearly shows an absence of God, doesn't it? In scripture we see God use the elements of the Earth to both decimate the human race, as well as, save His chosen people (crossing the Red Sea). So how does that work?

To start looking at this mystery, we need to look at the big picture, and of course, start in the beginning. After God had created the Earth and all that inhabited it, *"God saw everything that he had made, and indeed, it was very good." (Gen 1: 31).*

> *"By the very nature of creation, material being is endowed with its own stability, truth, and excellence, its own order and laws."* Each of the various creatures, willed in its own being, reflects in its own way a ray of God's infinite wisdom and goodness.
>
> CCC 339

By the design of God, the world was to be stable, orderly, and a reflection of God. The fall of man, and the introduction of sin into the world, destabilized the world God created. This allowed disaster and evil to have permanent residence in our world. Evil is not a creation of God and so, by itself, does not reflect the goodness of God, but just like how God can use us sinful people to change the world, so too, can He use evil to bring good into the world.

> *The fact that God permits physical and even moral evil is a mystery that God illuminates by his son Jesus Christ*

> *who died and rose to vanquish evil. Faith gives us the certainty that God would not permit an evil if he did not cause a good to come from that very evil, by ways that we shall fully know only in eternal life.*
>
> *CCC 324*

Whenever we are faced with tragedy and sorrow, our mind is immediately drawn into the strong emotions of fear, sadness, and anger. We allow our emotions to get the best of us, and we become blind to God's presence, even in times of devastation. Go back and look at the tornado picture of the town's destruction. What was the first thing you saw? The rubble, the destroyed car, or the trees were stripped of any sign of life. Now look deeper into the picture and what do you see behind the destruction? Behind the rubble stands our church. Untouched, and standing as a beacon over the devastated town.

The great challenge is finding the good that God has created out of tragedy. If a parent is diagnosed with cancer, we can identify that that is a tragedy, but what if God uses that as an opportunity to bring feuding siblings back together? If a town is destroyed by a storm, the loss is great but the strength that the community finds in one another makes it stronger than before. If a church is ridiculed by the scandals of men, the response to protect, defend, and help innocent victims makes the church greater and safer than it was before. Just like in the picture of the rubble, we must look past the evil and search for God in everything we encounter.

It's not going to be easy, and we are going to have our doubts. Our faith is always going to be tested, and every one of us will have moments where we ask, "Is this actually leading to something, or maybe this life is all we get and I should focus more on me?" Evil can lead us to doubt, but doubt can lead us to knowledge and understanding. That is how God works in our lives. Our moments of doubt are opportunities to learn more about God and strengthen our relationship with him. Whenever we are faced with doubt, look at the Divine Mercy portrait and pray, "Jesus, I trust in you."

This book isn't designed to be a one-stop fix, but more as a fuel gauge for our faith journey. When our faith is low, we need to go back to the beginning and strengthen our understanding of who God is. If there's room left in the tank, then we need to fill it up with prayer and our love for God. Once the tank is full, we are finally equipped to accomplish the final step in building our faith, and that is going out into the world and serving God's people.

Serve God

Have you ever tried to build a house of cards? Well, there's only one way to start and that is at the bottom. If we want to build more than just a basic teepee, we need to have a plan and establish a solid foundation. The tricky part is getting vertical. You see with each level, you start to realize how important it is to have a solid foundation to build on. The higher you get, the greater chance for failure because with each level there is more chance of making a mistake. We can fall into traps of rushing, leaving our tower vulnerable, and running the risk of our tower completely collapsing.

If our house of cards does come tumbling down, it's back to square one. Sometimes we can become discouraged and instead of building up we simply build out. The fear of "wasting" our time knowing we are just going to collapse in the end, deters us from pursuing our goals of building this grand house.

This is the challenge we face when building our relationship with God. In this book, we have focused on the first two steps of getting to know and love God. As we reach each step, we are vertically elevating our spiritual life, but we can identify that it is fragile. We are worried our weak spots will leave us vulnerable to falling into sin and away from God. This can lead us to get comfortable just staying in step one, and telling ourselves the lie, that it is "good enough."

As we build our lives we need to fortify our foundation as we keep reaching higher. We can't stop reading scripture because we developed a daily prayer life, but instead, our prayer life must be built on that commitment to knowing God better. It may be hard to hear but it only gets harder the farther along we get. The devil doesn't waste his time on the sinful but strives to corrupt the righteous. As we strive towards step three, we always must be cautious of the foundation we have built up. We must continue growing our knowledge and love of God as we go out to serve God's people.

It's not going to be easy. Just like the house of cards, we will have our flaws. Maybe we have a few bent or crinkled cards in our deck, but that's what makes your house yours. Knowing how fragile it is, we must be vigilant in protecting it from those who want to cause it harm, either due to jealousy or anger. Nothing would make them happier than to see it come crashing down.

When we feel that our home is complete (although it never is), we must not boast about our accomplishments. Instead, we must look to help others. Just like someone once showed you how to build, we too must help others build that first teepee. Help them when it falls, help them when they have doubts, and encourage them when they fear failure.

Fear

Fear … (queue Batman voice). It is safe to say that our fears are constantly developing and changing. Think back to when you were a kid and what your biggest fears were. Rollercoasters, spiders, the dark, water, … girls. For me, it was just talking in general. My friends always teased me that I never spoke until the 7th grade, and they weren't wrong. I was very shy, quiet, and just never spoke up. Now, I lecture at church, teach religious education to high schoolers, lead religious discussions for our Knights of Columbus council, and write books. I found my voice and now I use it.

So what changed? Well, starting in sixth grade, a few of my friends and I joined the speech team. My brother was a senior on the speech team and encouraged us to try it. I ended up doing it for a total of four years before calling it quits. The category that I was in was storytelling … shocker, I know. The whole goal was to take these old fairytale stories, use voices, gestures, and be the best at presenting the story. I was terrible. I could barely talk in math class, but now, I had to be an evil stepmother, a tiger, and a princess, while coming up with five different voices and that's just for one of the 15 different stories we had to prepare. I wasn't very good, but I guess I wasn't doing it to be the best storyteller but to better myself. By the time I got to 9th grade, I was comfortable speaking in front of people, and I was able to have normal conversations. My personality was developing and I had overcome my fear of speaking in general.

When we talk about fear, it's the belief that something may be harmful, threatening, or dangerous to us. Most of the time our fear derives from the unknown aspect of something. We are scared of the dark or water, because who knows what creatures may be lurking in them. We believe that what we can't see, can harm us. Now as we all get older, our fears are going to adapt, but the core will stay the same.

    As an adult, our fears are things that are out of our control. A study performed by Chapman University in 2022 confirms that.[29] What was the number one fear of adults in America? Government corruption. What goes on behind closed doors and how it has a direct impact on my life, my future, and my children? Other fears on this list are; nuclear war, pollution, financial collapse, and the death or illness of a loved one. When we were kids, we thought it would be great to be an adult because then we would get to make the rules and control our lives, yet modern adults find themselves controlled by their phones, politicians, news agencies, and peer pressure. Who is in control of your life?

    If we are obsessed with social media on our phones, we fear missing out on life because we see everyone else's highlight reels. We view our life as more of a failure because we don't have trips to post about or fancy Michelin-star meals. Politicians are constantly stirring up the fear of their opponents by promising that if they are elected, the world knows it will collapse. Like any salesman, all your problems can be solved by sending me your vote and your dollar. If you watch the news you will be "informed" of all the tragedy that fills the world and country. Wildfires, police violence, shark

---

[29] Grevin, Christian. "The Top 10 Fears in America 2022 - Did Your Fears Make the List?" The Voice of Wilkinson, October 14, 2022.

attacks, natural disasters, school shootings, political scandals, car accidents, arson, pollution, virus outbreak, money fraud, fear, Fear, FEAR! Modern news is a glimpse into the world, but only through the lens of fear. Wanting to draw you into the chaos of our world making you feel helpless. Don't worry though because we will end with a 30-second clip of a kid donating his old bike just so you feel a little bit better about the world. Now, I'm not saying that you shouldn't watch the news but stay informed locally. As tragic as the news out of New York City may be, it has little impact on you if you live in a small town in Minnesota, rural Texas, or a west coast city. Violence and corruption in foreign places only lead us to fear the world around us.

> *Scoundrels concoct evil,*
> *And their speech is like a scorching fire.*
>
> *A perverse person spreads strife,*
> *and a whisperer separates close friends.*
>
> *The violent entice their neighbours,*
> *and lead them in a way that is not good.*
>
> *Proverbs 16:27-29*

    Our lives are overly saturated with information, and the desire to know all the gossip and details. That's why this new generation of social networking, political corruption, and 24-hour news cycles is harming our minds. We fill our minds with so much useless information, that we can't enjoy our own lives but instead are constantly living to watch other people live theirs. I know what you're thinking, "We need to know what's going on in the world to protect ourselves." My response to that is, do you think you're the first person in human history to deal with a corrupt world? Is this a new fear?

Peter and the disciples saw their beloved friend and Master get killed by the local power. He was mocked, humiliated, beaten until He could barely walk, and then forced to drag His cross through the streets. Nailed onto a cross, displayed for the world to see so that the Romans could make an example of him. While He hung there, He experienced hours of the most excruciating pain as His lungs slowly collapsed until He handed over His spirit.

Fear controlled the apostles after the crucifixion. Their friend was murdered, their leader (Peter) had denied Him before His death, Judas, their friend betrayed him, and the city was looking for them to put them through the same thing. So what did they do? They hid in the upper room. Just like we hide in our homes behind our phones and TVs scared of the world. Scared of the people around us. *"The doors of the house where the disciples had met were locked for fear of the Jews." (John 20:19)*

Is this a reality we just have to live with? That the world is a dark and scary place filled with demons, violence, and scandal? Is there truly no hope for the world? The reality is that fear develops in the absence of God. That is what the apostles experienced after the death of Jesus. Without God, they feared the world. Our modern fear is a wedge between us and God that was placed by the devil himself to keep us separated. We allow the devil to distort the image of God, allowing us to distort the view of the world He created. It's the same fear Adam and Eve introduced when they sinned.

> *Then the eyes of both were opened, and they knew that they were naked; and they sewed fig leaves together and made loincloths for themselves. They heard the sound of the Lord walking in the garden ... and the man and his wife hid themselves from the presence of the Lord God among the trees of the garden. But the Lord God called to the man, and said to him, 'Where are you?' He said, 'I heard the sound of you in the garden, and I was afraid, because I was naked; and I hid myself.'*
>
> *Genesis 3:7-10*

From the very beginning, the devil has accomplished his goal of separating God from man, and continues to separate us with modern "fruit". Social media, politicians, and news, all promise that the more we know our *"eyes will be opened, and you will be like God, knowing good and evil (Gen 3:5)*. This modern "fruit" keeps our minds stagnant, and a stagnant mind is the devil's playground. Keeping us lazy, addicted, and obsessed with meaningless information allows the devil to keep a wedge between us and God. Like an idle car, on and running, but going nowhere.

How can we remove this wedge? Well, exactly what we have already talked about in this book. Love is our freedom from the devil's works. Love from our friends and our families drives our fears away. It's the devil telling us that the Bible isn't worth reading, and it's his lies that say the saints lived boring lives. It's by his evil design that we are attracted to music, tv, and gossip instead of a devout prayer life. For when we love God, He drives the devil back, and with him, our fears.

Going back to the apostles hiding in the upper room, what changed their hearts?

> *Suddenly from Heaven, there came a sound like the rush of a violent wind, and it filled the entire house where they were sitting. ... All of them were filled with the Holy Spirit and began to speak in other languages, ...Now there were devout Jews from every nation under Heaven living in Jerusalem ... But Peter, standing with the eleven. Raised his voice and addressed them.*
>
> *Acts 2:2,4-5,14*

On that first Pentecost, the Holy Spirit drove out the fear from the apostles. In doing so, the Catholic faith was born, and Christianity began to spread to every corner of the globe. Their bravery is the reason that over 2.6 billion Christians are believing in God today[30]. That same love that drove out the apostles' fear is still flowing in us all today, but we have to untap it.

---

[30] Zach Dawes Jr Managing editor for news and opinion at Good Faith Media. "Global Christian Population Projected to Reach 3.3 Billion by 2050." Good Faith Media, February 14, 2023.

The apostles faced their challenges. They were arrested, and persecuted for their beliefs, but they were not deterred from preaching the Word of God. God prepared the apostles as He prepares us today for all of our battles. With God by your side, there is no challenge that you can't face head-on.

With the power of the Holy Spirit, the apostles went from hiding because of the fear of death, to laying down their lives for the love of Christ. Here's how the lives of the apostles' ended;

Peter - Crucified (Upside down)
Paul - Beheaded
Andrew - Crucified (X shape)
Thomas - Thrust with spears
Philip - Crucified
Matthew - Stabbed
Bartholomew - Flayed and Beheaded
James the Greater - Stabbed
James the Lesser - Stoned
Simon - Crucified
Matthias -Crucified
Thaddeus - Filled with arrows
John - Old Age[31]

---

[31] Roach, Becky, Guest Post, St. John Vianney, St. Thomas More, Pope Francis, and Catholic Saint. "Infographic: What Happened to the Apostles after Jesus Died?" Catholic, March 12, 2018.

Although, the apostles were fearless, they weren't invincible, but they knew that their love of God was stronger than death. There is no greater evidence that the Resurrection of Christ is true when you see how many people are willing to lay down their lives for Christ and His church. In the last 2,000 years, over 70 million individuals have given up their lives to stand up for their faith in Jesus[32].

In America, we should always be protected to practice and defend our faith. Although we may never be in a position to give up our lives, we are certain to be mocked, ridiculed, harassed, and judged. We will be called hateful, bigots, bible thumpers, homophobes, transphobes, and many other hateful things. We must stand strong in our love of God, and conquer our fears. Our world is a spiritual battleground and we are the soldiers fighting for God.

> *Rid yourselves, therefore, of all malice, and all guile, insincerity, envy, and all slander … Come to him, a living stone, though rejected by mortals yet chosen and precious in God's sight, and like living stones, let yourselves be built into a spiritual house, to be a holy priesthood, to offer spiritual sacrifices acceptable to God through Jesus Christ … But you are a chosen race, a royal priesthood, a holy nation, God's own people. In order that you may proclaim the mighty acts of him who called you out of darkness into his marvelous light.*

---

[32] Gzurlo. "Christian Martyrdom: Who? Why? How?" Gordon Conwell, September 27, 2019.

1 Peter 2:1, 4-5,9

But now thus says the LORD, he who created you, O Jacob, he who formed you, O Israel: "Fear not, for I have redeemed you; I have called you by name, you are mine.

Isaiah 43:1

The Rich Man and Lazarus

'There was a rich man who was dressed in purple and fine linen and who feasted sumptuously every day. And at his gate lay a poor man named Lazarus, covered with sores, who longed to satisfy his hunger with what fell from the rich man's table; even the dogs would come and lick his sores. The poor man died and was carried away by the Angels to be with Abraham. The rich man also died and was buried. In Hades, where he was being tormented, he looked up and saw Abraham far away with Lazarus by his side. He called out, "Father Abraham, have mercy on me, and send Lazarus to dip the tip of his finger in water and cool my tongue; for I am in agony in these flames." But Abraham said, "Child, remember that during your lifetime you received your good things, and Lazarus in like manner evil things; but now he is comforted here, and you are

in agony. Besides all this, between you and us a great chasm has been fixed, so that those who might want to pass from here to you cannot do so, and no one can cross from there to us." He said, "Then, father, I beg you to send him to my father's house for I have five brothers - that he may warn them, so that they will not also come into this place of torment." Abraham replied, "They have Moses and the prophets; they should listen to them." He said, "No, father Abraham; but if someone goes to them from the dead, they will repent." He said to him, "If they do not listen to Moses and the prophets, neither will they be convinced even if someone rises from the dead."'

Luke 16: 19-31

As we read this story a lot is going on and many different aspects to focus on. First off, we see that our two main characters are Lazarus, who is received into Heaven when he dies, and the rich man, who is doomed to eternity in hell.

The relationship between these two is non-existent and Lazarus is just a poor man who lies outside the rich man's gate. One thing to note in this Gospel passage is that the rich man never harms Lazarus at any point. There is no mention of him abusing, spitting, or mocking Lazarus as he lay outside of his gate. So why is his punishment hell?

The answer is quite simple, and we see references to this similar situation throughout the Gospel.

For I was hungry and you gave me food, I was thirsty and you gave me drink, I was a stranger and you welcomed me.

Matthew 25:35

    This parable, and what Jesus talks about in the Gospel of Matthew is a warning about what is expected of us in our day-to-day lives. We are called to a life of action and to focus on more than ourselves. Even when he is suffering in hell and he sees Lazarus, the rich man asks Abraham for Lazarus to help him instead of asking for forgiveness. When we live selfish lives, we put up roadblocks to anyone else that might slow us down on our way to our desires. It's human nature to put ourselves first and to ignore any inconvenience. How often do we neglect to improve someone else's day because it isn't important to us? Where, even simply, putting effort into making someone else smile becomes a self-proclaimed burden on our shoulders? Pride just like all sin puts "I" at the center.[33]

    The sin of the rich man is neglect and selfishness. To him, Lazarus is a nuisance that doesn't have any impact on his life, and he just ignores him. His lack of action to help Lazarus was what doomed him to damnation.

    The final aspect I want to focus on with this story is when the rich man asks Abraham to send Lazarus and warn his brothers to spare them from this torment. Abraham

---

[33] Karen. "Sin Has an I in the Middle." Sharing Horizons, April 10, 2017.

denies him and says that they have the prophets and they have their warning. This isn't good enough for the rich man and says, but surely, if someone were to rise from the dead, they would believe. What Abraham says is the most alarming part, *"If they do not listen to Moses and the prophets, neither will they be convinced even if someone rises from the dead."*

Now, this is starting to sound familiar. What Abraham warns about is correct. Look at where we are today. We have the prophets, apostles, saints, and even God himself, who came to walk this Earth to live among us, teach us how to live, and died for our sins. To take it one step further, He rose from the dead to show us that there is victory over death. Even with all this evidence, we have never been farther from God as a country and as a world. Today more than ever, people don't believe in God, and even those who call themselves Christians, fail to believe in His teachings.

> *'Not everyone who says to me, "Lord, Lord", will enter the kingdom of heaven, but only one who does the will of my Father in heaven ... Then I will declare to them, "I never knew you; go away from me, you evildoers."*
>
> *(Matt 7:21-23)*

I know this is true because if we, as God's children, truly knew who He was, and what He did for us, every pew would be full on Sundays with lines out the door, every knee would drop in His presence in the Eucharist, and every heart would weep for His love and forgiveness at the Mass. I fear that if we don't make the day-to-day effort to improve our relationship with God, we will all be doomed to eternity in hell. Every time we ignore our neighbors in need, we are ignoring God. Every time we put ourselves first, we put God last. The people we interact with on a day-to-day basis may not be physically hungry, but spiritually, they may be starving. How often do we get down to the deep question about how someone is feeling instead of simply chatting about the weather and how the local teams are performing? How often do we show those around us that we care and that they are loved?

Sharing the Faith

As a catechist, there is at least one guaranteed question, "How do we get to Heaven?" Although there are a lot of different answers that would satisfy their minds, I have always rested on one answer. "The easiest way to get to Heaven is to turn around and bring someone else with you."

But how are we supposed to do that? If I even bring up religion around friends or family, it's the easiest way to shut down a party. People start looking at you funny, redirect the conversation, or just walk away. How am I supposed to share the faith without coming off as pushy, or weird? Am I supposed to go door to door until I find someone who will listen?

Evangelizing is a very challenging obstacle in our faith. Mostly because we get discouraged as soon as we face failure, or what we assume is a failure. Sometimes, we take the priest's final blessing at the end of Mass, "go forth", literally, and try to bring it up to everyone we meet. Maybe we are grocery shopping and we bring up that Sunday's Gospel to the cashier. What? No response besides paper or plastic? How about you see your neighbors on a walk and you start sharing the message from the priest's homily? 'Minnesota Nice' says they have to acknowledge you, nod their head, and say "That's nice" before walking away from you. Maybe you grab a free book from church and want to give it to your friend, but they reject it because they just don't have time to start a new book right now. How are we supposed to share the faith when people don't share our excitement or enthusiasm? When busy lives take up all their free time?

Maybe we want to try and cast a wider net so we try to be a glimmer of light on social media. Sharing posts, suggesting books, encouraging people to start listening to podcasts, or faith-focused videos for people to watch. Yet, once again, we are met with very little enthusiasm. It's too easy for people to see Jesus and just keep on scrolling. Don't take it personally, but social media is just not where people go to learn about God. For example, if I post a beautiful picture of my daughter, that picture is going to soar past 100 likes, heart, and other fancy emojis. Now what do you think happens when I make a post about Jesus? 18, but if you subtract my wife and closest family, maybe 11 people stopped to like that post. That doesn't even mean they read it.

Maybe it was just the nice picture I found on the internet that they liked.

So if I can't just post about my love for God, and I can't shout to the world about Him, how is anyone supposed to reignite their faith in Christ? How can I help others love God as much as I do? You need to show them what they are missing. Let your actions show them what it is like to be in communion with God. If we want people to love God as we do, we can't walk around this world moping wherever we go. Our souls should be filled with the Holy Spirit, and the joy in our hearts should fill this world with light. Now I get it, there are days when we just need to get through the day without completely falling apart, but even on our worst days, we need to show others how God gets us through. Always finding the bright side, and staying positive.

What do people think when they see you? How does the stranger see you when you are at the grocery store? Do we smile throughout the day? How about going out of our way to help others, even if it slows us down by 2 minutes? Do we show charity and forgiveness to strangers that we will never see again? To be honest, do we allow ourselves to be weird or different in the eyes of the public norm? If there is anything this book should show us, it's that we don't want to be what the world views as normal. Out of the billions of people that have lived on this planet, God decided that it needed YOU! It's time to allow the world to see the best and brightest side of you. The person that God always envisioned you to be. *"All people are born as originals but many die as photocopies"*[34] *(Blessed Carlso Acutis)*

---

[34] Alyssa Murphy "17 Inspiring Quotes from Carlo Acutis." NCR.

It's time to be a little bit different. People are going to notice and will probably wonder, "What is their problem?" Some people will judge us for being happy, but we can't let this deter us from our mission.

> *Do not fear what they fear, and do not be intimidated, but in your hearts sanctify Christ as Lord. Always be ready to make your defense to anyone who demands from you an account of the hope that is in you; yet do it with gentleness and reverence.*
>
> 1 Peter 3: 14-16

Whether people turn away from us, laugh, gossip, or sneer, do not let them discourage your heart. Show them love and mercy with a kind heart. The joy and love we show to others could just be the spark they needed to reignite their faith.

How often do we invite people to Mass? Do you ever invite a stranger you passed on the streets to join you? A friend who you know hasn't been to church in a long time? How about a family member who has fallen out of their faith because of anger with God? How often do we show everyone around us that the doors to the kingdom are wide open, and even better, they are invited to the banquet inside? Yet, many feel unwelcome.

When I was in college, one of my roommates wasn't a Christian. I would say he probably lined up with a more agnostic belief. On the rare event that both of us stayed in Brookings for the weekend, I made a habit of at least sending him an invite. He would always say, "Thanks but not this time." It didn't hurt my feelings, but it was important to me that he knew it wasn't a members-only celebration. A few years later, I was dressed up for Holy Thursday Mass, and as I was walking to church, I passed the nearby low-income apartment building. A man was playing with his kids and asked me, "Man, what are you so dressed up for?" I laughed and said, "It was holy week and I was heading to Mass." "ON A THURSDAY!?", the man shouted and I started to laugh. I told him, "It doesn't start for another 30 minutes. I'm sure you can make it in time." He politely declined and said, "I'll have to check it out sometime."

One way to look at it is I had a 0% success rate at getting anybody besides myself to church. Now the other way is I started a ripple effect in someone's life. In both cases, they are people that I haven't seen in years. Who knows where their life has brought them, and if a simple invite changed everything down the road?

In Matthew Kelly's book *holy moments*, he talks about one of the best pieces of advice he ever received. "You will only ever see less than one percent of the impact you have on people's lives."[35] We can't evangelize by trying to make ourselves feel accomplished. If that is our goal, we are completely backward. To evangelize is to help OTHERS. It doesn't matter if I receive a gift of gratitude, or a thank you card in the mail. I may never see the impact I had on the lives of all the students we've taught, or the people that read my

---

[35] Kelly, Matthew. *Holy moments: A handbook for the rest of Your life.* North Palm Beach, FL: Blue Sparrow, 2022.

book. Instead, let us pray like Desmond Doss, the hero of Hacksaw Ridge, "Lord, help me get one more."[36]

We were discussing this topic at our Knights of Columbus meeting and I asked all the men a question. "If you were walking over a bridge and you saw a giant rock, what would you do?" The best part of a men's group is our male instinct was all the same. "You throw it into the water." If I were to throw a large rock into the creek below, it would make a huge splash, and waves would flow from it until it hit each bank. Next, if I grabbed a small rock that fits in the palm of my hand, what would happen if I dropped it? No big splash, but as it submerged into the water, ripples would spread across the water to each bank. Finally, I grab the smallest pebble wedged in the grooves on the bottom of my shoe. As soon as I drop it, I lose sight of it until I see it disturb the water. Even with its limited size, ripples begin to spread to each bank. It doesn't matter if we change one life or thousands, every action we take has a massive ripple effect. Whether we make an impact as an individual, a community, or as a whole church, we can alter the world around us one life at a time. That is how we can change the world.

> *I alone cannot change the world, but I can cast a stone across the waters to create many ripples.*
>
> Saint Mother Teresa[37]

---

[36] Schenkkan, Robert. *Hacksaw Ridge*, 2016.

[37] Teresa, and Matthew Kelly. *Do something beautiful for God: The essential teachings of mother teresa: 365 daily reflections*. North Palm Beach, FL: Blue Sparrow, 2019.

Going back to Matthew Kelly's book, *holy moments,* he brings up the idea of spiritual multiplication. This is putting numbers to our ripple effect. If I can inspire 3 people and those three people find three more people, it doesn't take long before 1,000,000 people are impacted because of you. If we do the math and do this exercise 13 times, where every new person finds 3 more, we would eclipse 2.3 million. Your impact on someone else's life can have an exponential impact on the world, and the only thing stopping you is you.

There is no shortage of opportunities to evangelize in this world. If we use Matthew Kelly's goal of sharing your faith with 3 people, I would challenge you to start with these 3 specifically;

1. Family member
2. Parishioner who has stopped attending Mass
3. Neighbor, friend, or stranger from outside the church

The core of our evangelizing has to start from within. Just like we need to keep our spiritual lights bright, we need to keep the light bright in our church.

It shouldn't be understated that we live in a spiritually hungry world. Not much different than the world Christ entered into. Everyone around us is searching for answers and guidance. Of the four Gospels, there is only one miracle that appears in all of them, and that is the feeding of the 5,000. How did Christ view the crowd, and why is it such an important miracle?

As he went ashore he saw a great crowd; and he had compassion for them, because they were like sheep without a shepherd; and he began to teach them many things.

Mark 6:34

Compassion! The world is filled with broken people. We all are broken from the start with original sin, and with each passing day, we get more cracks and blemishes. When we introduce people to God, we are telling them that there is a path to happiness, joy, eternal love, and a God who will take your broken pieces. In Japan, they have a form of pottery called Kintsugi (golden joinery). In this practice, they take broken pieces of pottery and put them back together using gold, silver, or platinum. "It treats breakage and repair as part of the history of an object, rather than something to disguise."[38] It becomes even more beautiful than it was when it was in "perfect" condition.

Are you ready to answer the call? When the Lord asks you, *"Do you love me?"* How will you respond when He says, *"Feed my Sheep" (John 21:17)*

---

[38] Bartlett, Christy. "Kintsugi – Art of Repair." Traditional Kyoto.

As I Have Done For You

While I was going to school at South Dakota State, my brother and I would always get 'all-session passes' to the conference tournament in Sioux Falls for our men's and women's basketball teams. It was a fun four-day stretch watching 14 basketball games and cheering on our squads. It's safe to say that we, Jackrabbit fans, have been spoiled with our basketball programs over the years when it comes to conference success. I better move on to the point or else the rest of this book is just going to be about SDSU athletics.

So what does a basketball tournament have to do with our faith? Nothing, but after that tournament, as I jumped on the interstate to head back to Brookings, I was flipping through the radio stations and caught myself stopping on a Christian channel. I have no idea what the station was, but in the 5 minutes that I listened to it, I heard something that has stuck with me to this day, "There is no obstacle that God hasn't previously prepared you for." It was such a comforting statement. When we face judgment, persecution, anger, or fear, we should find comfort in knowing that God doesn't throw us into a battle that we can not persevere through, or that He hasn't prepared us for. Maybe that's the gift of being calm, or the ability to brush off someone's rude remarks to you.

> *The Lord is my strength and my shield; in him my heart trusts; so I am helped, and my heart exults, and with my song I give thanks to him.*

Psalm 28:7

As I have gotten older, I realize that it isn't just the hard times that God prepares us for. If we look at the many blessings in our lives that we don't feel worthy to receive, has God not prepared our hearts for the good as well? Many don't feel prepared to be husbands or fathers. That moment of, "Am I ready to have someone else rely on me? Can I take care of someone else?" Yet, the nerves of getting married rush away as soon as you see your bride or the anxiety of being a parent disappears as soon as you hold that child. No longer is your mind flooded with the mental checklist of what needs to be done to "be prepared" and yet the calming presence of God whispering in your ear saying, "You got this." We need to find comfort in the Lord. God shows us love, mercy, compassion, and grace, not because we deserve it, but because as any good father, He is setting the example for His children.

Throughout this book, I have emphasized the importance of living a sacramental life, and being consistent at receiving the sacraments. It is through the sacraments that God sets the example of how to love one another because that is how He loves us.

Through Baptism, we are welcomed into a community, and shown how we should be welcoming. God forgives us in Reconciliation just like we are to forgive others. The Holy Eucharist reminds us of God's greatest sacrifice, and how we need to make sacrifices for all those that we meet. At Confirmation, we are filled with the courage of the Holy Spirit to go forth into the world fearlessly. Matrimony and Holy Orders remind us that we are part of an unbreakable covenant where we are one with God as we are one with our spouse. Anointing of the Sick, God comforts the ailing, just as we should care for those who are sick and near death.

God shows us how to love, and that is a love that every person deserves. Just like how we have focused on getting to know, love, and serve God, so too shall we do the same with His people. Our relationships have the same formula. If I am not willing to continue learning more about my wife each day, am I committed to her? If I always put my own needs first and live a selfish marriage, do I love my wife? All of our relationships require effort, and it is up to us to be vigilant every day to fulfill the love that we are called to give.

If you need a reminder I would encourage you to do one simple thing. In our bedroom above the door, we have a crucifix hanging. As I get up every morning I look up and I am reminded of how much love God has for me. So much love, that we were worth dying for. I pray, "Lord help me love like you and help me be your light to the world."

Before Christ was hung on the cross, He sat down with His friends for one final meal. As they gathered around the table, Jesus removed His robe and tied a towel around His waist. He then began to wash their feet. The God who made the entire universe in a flash, who breathed life into man, and has gone forth to build a kingdom for His followers, became a servant.

So if I, your Lord and Teacher, have washed your feet, you also ought to wash one another's feet. For I have set you an example, that you also should do as I have done for you.

John 13:14-15

SHINE!

Catholics tend to cringe when the term "works" gets brought up in a religious conversation. If you ask anybody who isn't Catholic, it's usually on their short list of objections to the church. Catholics always hear the same objections. "You worship Mary ... You don't believe you can confess directly to God ... You have to earn your spot in Heaven", all are misconceptions of the Catholic faith. So the question is do Catholics believe you have to earn your way into Heaven by good works?

The quickest answer is no because we are saved by the grace of God who suffered and died for us. My follow-up question is that, if we need to know who God is, and love God to receive His grace, then wouldn't the result of that love be to share it with as many people as possible? Shouldn't our relationship with God influence how we treat and care for those around us? If we find ourselves in a state of joy because of the grace of God, shouldn't that be something we share with everyone we meet?

When we look at the world in 2023, there are over 8 billion people that live on this planet. Apart from that population, there are 2.6 Billion Christians (33%). That's a third of the population that continues the faith of the saints, the martyrs, and 12 Jewish men from the middle east. What if the 12 stayed cowering in the upper room and never spread the word? Would Jesus just have become another myth like Zeus or Jupiter? Think of all the good that Christianity has done over the last 2,000 years. Think of the scientific discoveries, hospitals, schools, and charities that would have never happened. By God's design, the Holy Spirit worked through the apostles and has worked through the church for 2,000 years, all the way to you. The same Spirit lives in YOU! Let it shine.

> 'For it is as if a man, going on a journey, summoned his servants and entrusted them; to one he gave five talents ($$$), to another two, to another one, to each according to his ability. Then he went away. The one who had received the five talents went off at once and traded with them, and made five more talents. ... But the one who had received the one talent went off and dug a hole in the ground and hid his master's money. After a long time the master of those servants came and settled accounts with them. Then the one who had received five talents came forward, bringing five more talents, saying "Master, you handed over to me five more talents; see, I have made five more talents." His master said to him, "Well done, good and trustworthy servant; you have been trustworthy in a few things, I will put you in charge of many things; enter into the joy of your master." ... Then the one who had received one talent also came forward, saying, "Master, I knew that

> *you were a harsh man ... so I was afraid, and I went and hid your talent in the ground. Here you have what is yours." But his master replied, "You wicked and lazy servant! ... As for this worthless servant, throw him into the outer darkness,*
>
> Matthew 25:14-30

As Christians, our inheritance is God's love and mercy. Whether we are born rich into the faith, or find Him later in life, we are all given this special gift. There is no greater inheritance than the knowledge and love of God. As we see in the parable, the wise servant multiplied his talents and it was pleasing to the Master. Where the servant with the smallest talent, hid out of fear and angered his Master.

One of the biggest faults in our world today is spiritual laziness. How often do we decide that "we" know what is right and wrong instead of God? How often do we bend the rules to satisfy our self-interests? Do we take God's inheritance for granted and waste our lives thinking that the work is done? When we bury our talents we are making a mockery of the crucifixion. If we can look at the crucifix while sitting on our couch and think, "Thank goodness for that guy", then what are we doing? Many Christians believe that by faith alone we are saved. I worry that when we live a life of faith alone, we think that just because we believe in God, we are free to miss Mass a few times, skip the sacraments, and live a sinful life because nothing is impossible for God right? Although that is correct, I would call that an abusive relationship. We are saved by God alone, but if we bury our faith, then we will be cast out into the darkness.

> *'You are the light of the world. A city built on a hill cannot be hidden. No one after lighting a lamp puts it under the bushel basket, but on the lampstand, and it gives light to all in the house. In the same way, let your light shine before others, so that they may see your good works and give glory to your Father in Heaven.*
>
> *Matthew 5:14-16*

SHINE! You are the light of the world. Do you ever find yourself complaining that the world isn't the way it used to be, or that our culture (If we even have one anymore) is in the gutter? How many Christians see church attendance dwindle year after year and think that the problem is the "others" have lost their way? The reason we feel this way is that too many have buried their faith and covered up their lamps. How is the world supposed to function when we allow the world to be infested with darkness?

How can I make a difference? How can I make my light shine? If you haven't been to Easter Vigil lately, that's the Saturday night Mass we always feel is way longer than it actually is, you should make it a habit to always go. The Easter Vigil contains one of my favorite moments in the entire church year. As we begin the celebration, we start in darkness. The only source of light is coming from the back of the church, where the Priest has a large fire and the Paschal candle lit. The congregation, concluding their lenten season of repentance, stands in the dark church holding unlit candles. Through our sin, we have allowed our lights to be extinguished.

Then something beautiful takes place. The priest/deacon starts to process with the Paschal candle professing, "The Light of Christ, The Light of Christ, The Light of Christ." As he processes one by one the laity light their candles. From the one source of light, they pass the light to their children and their neighbors. By the time the Paschal candle makes it to the front of the church, the whole church is glowing with individual lights.

How beautiful a sight when everyone's light shines? The church is beaming with light, and the darkness of Lent is no more. Sin and death have been defeated with love and life taking its place. That should be our goal every day. To take that light that we have received from God and share it with everyone around us. One person at a time, we can light up this world.

Between my parents and grandparents, I have been witness to wonderful marriages. As a kid, I watched my parents be genuine best friends and never waste a moment to remind each other that they love each other. One of the simple gestures that my father always did was to turn the garage lights on. Why? If you ask my parents, if you come home and see a light on for you, that means that you are loved. This isn't a casual thing either. I've seen my mom's car coming down the road and having to yell at my dad that the garage light is off, and he will run down to make sure it gets turned on. Trust me she will notice. Even after 36 years of marriage, their love shines for each other.

So how can I shine in my community? The corporal and spiritual works of mercy are beautiful ways that we are instructed to help those suffering around us. Even if we are suffering ourselves, there is always someone who has it worse. Let's dive into the Corporal works of mercy.

Feed the hungry
- Help at a food shelter - make donations to your local food shelf - deliver prepared meals to the elderly.

Give drink to the thirsty
- Donate water after a major disaster - on a hot day, make sure that those working outside are properly hydrated, or those without shelter have something to drink.

Shelter the homeless
- Volunteer and donate to your nearest homeless shelter - donate time to help build shelters - make sure that shelters have plenty of beds, blankets, and pillows.

Visit the sick
- Donate blood - visit a nursing home and participate in activities with them - visit your home-bound neighbor or grandparent - throw a party for caregivers to show your appreciation for them.

Visit the prisoners
- See if there is a local ministry that visits prisoners - find a charity that donates presents to children who have parents in jail.

Bury the dead
- Visit cemeteries - pray for the dead - send cards to the families of the deceased.

Give alms to the poor
- Find areas in your life you can cut back costs, and give the difference to a charity - participate in the 'Lenten Rice Bowl' program.

USCCB[39]

When I went to school for education, we had to take numerous psychology classes. Although not a lot was retained, the one thing that I still find myself referring to is 'Maslow's Hierarchy of Needs'. For any individual to reach peak performance, they have to work up the pyramid. Starting with physical needs, safety, love and belonging, esteem, and then finally self-actualization.[40] If a kid is hungry, they don't care about photosynthesis. If a child has parents getting a divorce, they aren't worried about what the proper form of "there" they should be using. For our neighbors and communities to reach peak spiritual enlightenment, their physical needs have to be met. Are we meeting our neighbors where they are, instead of judging them for where they should be? Do we focus on our self-desires instead of our neighbor's basic needs?

---

[39] "The Corporal Works of Mercy." USCCB.

[40] Mcleod, Saul. "Maslow's Hierarchy of Needs Theory." Simply Psychology,

"Truly I tell you, just as you did it to one of the least of these my brothers, you did it to me."

Matthew 25:40

It's easy to watch someone else struggle. To be a bystander when someone is battling their demons. A lot of the time, we don't want to get involved, or we don't have the time to commit to helping them. Maybe I just don't like that guy and he probably deserved it. How often do we play the role of Simon of Cyrene during the crucifixion? Simon was a bystander in the large crowd watching and yelling as Jesus carried His cross through the streets of Jerusalem. He was seized and forced to help. How gracious do you think our Lord was at that moment to have someone help carry His cross, even if he didn't choose to?

Every person you meet is battling something or someone. It's much easier for us to be the judgemental bystander hiding in the crowd. Especially with social media, it's easy to linger in the comment section while someone is getting ridiculed and bullied. What would happen if we jumped in to help pick up someone else's cross? How much relief, and charity would that individual feel?

Let today be the first day that we strive to brighten our communities, and shine the light of Christ into the lives of those around us. If we strive to live every day as medics on a spiritual battleground, we hope that we will see God face to face someday and He will say, **"Well done my faithful servant."**

Epilogue

If there is anything from this book that I hope you walk away with, it is that our life is a long crooked journey. Whether we are starting this journey in high school, college, early in our marriage, or late in retirement, everything we have done has led us to God. St. Teresa of Avila is credited with saying, "God writes straight with crooked lines."[41] Although we may get disgruntled when relationships fall apart, jobs aren't what we expected them to be, or life just gets mundane, God is sitting upstairs saying, "Just you wait." His goal for us is far greater than we could ever understand.

I know what you are thinking, journeys are a lot easier if we have a map to guide us. I agree. If we start wandering through the woods alone, all we're going to accomplish is getting lost or killed along the way. We aren't meant to do this alone. We need to develop H.A.B.I.T.S. that guides us to God.

Another concept introduced to us during my wife's RCIA classes was the acronym 'H.A.B.I.T.S.'[42] If we can incorporate all six of these, we can live a more virtuous life. So let's dive in.

H - Holy Hour

---

[41] Grosso, John. "God Writes Straight with Crooked Lines." Diocese of Bridgeport, June 14, 2017.

[42] Gzurlo. "Christian Martyrdom: Who? Why? How?" Gordon Conwell, September 27, 2019.

- Daily Prayer Life

A - Accountability
- Taking responsibility for our actions and making a conscious choice of allowing God and others to help in accomplishing what is right.[43]

B - Bible
- Studying scripture and meditating on the word of God.

I - Invest
- Service in our community and charitable giving to those in need.

T - Tell
- Evangelize and tell all about Christ.

S - Sacraments
- Frequently participate in confession, and receive the Eucharist.

If we can commit to these spiritual habits, we will see a major difference in our lives. It is through these habits that we will increase our knowledge of God, and begin to love God the way He deserves, by serving God's people. We will have days where we struggle to pray, and we struggle to open up our Bibles, but we must continue striving to live holy lives. We can live saintly lives. All we have to do is never give up.

---

[43] "Magazines: Effective Communication – Footsteps 71." Tearfund Learn.

Other Books by Author

1910: Building a Legacy

1910 is a historical narration that follows the timeline of numerous immigrant Families coming to Southwest Minnesota. Along with their storylines, we see immigrants come through Ellis Island, colonize French Canada, and even some who have to bury their children at sea due to horrendous travel conditions. The sacrifice for all was great but their legacy prevails. As their children grow up they fight through drought, depression, wars, and death. We follow along with soldiers in WWll, sergeants in peaceful Germany, SW MN farmers, and teachers, and throughout the book, you get an incredibly comprehensive history of how humanity has progressed in SW MN from dirt floor houses in the prairie to modern farms. A story that is greatly relatable to all who have lived in Lyon County for over the past 100 years. Through stories of faith, love, and family we follow along with generations of Americans from the moment of their birth to their tragic death.

Homestead

A historical narration that follows the life of William Trulock who was a 19th-century English immigrant coming to America following the Civil War. Follow along his journey as he departs from England as a poor farm laborer to explore and discover the western border of the American Midwest. As he forges his path to establish a homestead he ventures too far west and finds himself in Dakota Territory. While in Dakota territory William discovers the culture and lifestyle of his native neighbors. Love, war, adventure, and exploration can all be found in Homestead.